A Consumer's Guide to Bad Taste

KITSCH

IN SYNC

A Consumer's Guide to Bad Taste

PETER WARD

Plexus, London

Copyright © 1991 by Peter Ward
Published by Plexus Publishing Limited
26 Dafforne Road
London SW17 8TZ
First printing 1991

Ward, Peter
  Kitsch in sync : a consumer's guide to bad taste
  I. Title
  700.9034

  ISBN 0 85965 152 5

Printed in Great Britain by Eagle Colourbooks Ltd
Cover and book design by Sandra Cowell

ACKNOWLEDGEMENTS

With grateful acknowledgements for photographs and illustrations: to e.t. Archive for the following: Herrenchimsee Castle, The Savoy Hotel and *Dr Johnson in Ante Room of Lord Chesterfield* by E.M. Ward with acknowledgement to the Tate Gallery; the Mansell Collection; the Hulton Deutsch Collection; Weimar Archive for *Mother and Child* by Liselotte Schramm and *The Awakening* by Richard Klein; The Bridgeman Art Library for the following: *Marilyn Diptych* by Andy Warhol, *Lobster Telephone* by Salvador Dali, with acknowledgement to Christie's, London, *Galatee* by Gustave Moreau with acknowledgment to M. Robert Lebel, Paris, *St. John the Baptist* by Puvis de Chavannes with acknowledgement to The Barber Institute, Birmingham, *In the Car, fur* by Roy Lichtenstein with acknowledgement to the Scottish National Gallery, *Campbell's Soup Can* by Andy Warhol with acknowledgement to The Saatchi Collection, *Got a Girl* by Peter Blake with acknowledgement to The Whitworth Art Gallery, Manchester; Pierre et Gilles for *The Medusa, St. Theresa* and *The Toreador*; BFI Stills, Posters and Designs; The Scala Cinema; Camera Press; Gered Mankowitz; Shaun Clarkson for *The Nancy Reagan Teapot*; Musee Nationale d'Art Moderne, Paris,

for Marcel Duchamp's *Urinal*; Popperfoto for *Soft Self Portrait* by Salvador Dali, and other photos; The Sonnabend Gallery for *Michael Jackson and Bubbles* by Jeff Koons; Riccardo Schicchi and Jeff Koons for *Illona on Top* by Jeff Koons; Memphis for *Ashoka* and *Casablanca* by Ettore Sotsass and *Colorado* by Marco Zanini; The Board of Trustees of the Victoria & Albert Museum; Niall McInerney; Channel Four; Central TV; Topham Picture Library; Peter Ward for all other photographs.

I am most indebted to the following people, without whom...Stephen Adamson for his invaluable contribution as editor (and more); Sandra Cowell for the design of the book, picture research and much support; Liz Eddison for picture research, Shaun Clarkson, Polly Grainger and Crestworth Ltd, James Lowe and Flying Duck Enterprises, Neil Mackenzie Matthews, Stephen Romney and his Too Damn Funky Collection, Dave Morley, Andy Inman and Bill Schriebman for supplying glittering photographs or the very best of tasteless objects to be photographed. Finally, my parents, and Phil Morrow and Paula Webb for helping me to avoid psychiatrists' couches and tranquillizer addiction whilst I was pulling this tome together.

CONTENTS

THE TRASH AESTHETIC

"In order to acquire bad taste one must first have very, very good taste"
John Waters

Fundamental to any understanding of kitsch is the idea of taste. Kitsch offers a perverse box of delights for its eclectically undiscriminating fans, but if you want to get to grips with the appeal of its garishly diverse seductions, you need to have some understanding of what taste is. In fact, if you haven't got jolly good taste, you won't appreciate kitsch at all (although you may surround yourself with it) Taste, of course, is the faculty we

Getting the bird. An unusual variation in brass on the china flying duck sets that originally became popular in the thirties. Flying ducks were one of the first common decorative household objects to be re-appropriated as kitsch - making the short flight from the flock wallpapers of the pre-war proletariat to the white-washed walls of the middle classes in the early seventies. Almost as much as cuddly animals, birds appeal to the worst in us (right).

possess for enjoying and discerning beauty. Like any exercise of judgement, decisions as to what is tasteful and what is not are based upon an amalgam of influences from different times and different places. The fact that people have widely differing likes and dislikes, or tastes, is as old as the hills, but both the application of the word 'taste', and the notion of an identifiable yardstick of aesthetic sensitivity only originated in seventeenth-century France. The concept evolved at a time when there was such a diversity of choice available that the high-minded considered it necessary to make a clear definition of what constituted the 'good' in art, design and literature. 'Taste' became the buzz word of polite conversation in the salons of Paris - the places where the intellectuals and artists of the time would gather and pontificate upon

6

The cognoscenti were an educated and wealthy mafia who gathered in the coffee houses, tea rooms, gentlemen's clubs and drawing rooms of eighteenth-century Europe and formulated the first rules of taste. Lord Chesterfield was a notable English example, and this painting by E.M. Ward shows Dr Johnson waiting in his ante room.

the science of beauty that we now know as aesthetics. After all, they had nothing more pressing to worry about.

At first 'good taste' was held to belong to only a very small number of people, a cognoscenti drawn from the clergy, education, the arts and wealthy society - by a strange coincidence the same people who were defining 'taste'. To these early aesthetes, taste was an immensely subtle and almost elusive notion. Like many small groups who think themselves uniquely possessed of the truth, they made grand claims for the power of their intellectual property. The Earl of Shaftesbury (1671-1713) described having taste as 'like having a new sense or faculty added to the soul' and Joseph Addison (1672-1719) thought that once universal taste was established, vice and ignorance would be banished from society (he was right, of course...).

From its haughty beginnings, the issue of taste good or bad has continually enraged people because of its subjective nature. The Romans saw this a long time before the polite rankles of seventeenth century society: a Latin tag, 'De gustibus non est disputandum', translated as 'There is no disputing about taste' is the earliest formation of the old chestnut, 'One man's meat is another man's poison'. For centuries this wrapped up the argument over the controversial matter of personal choice and opinion.

Even the early tastemakers could not agree on the essential nature of this marvellous quality. Some argued that aesthetic judgements were based upon mysterious, internal forces that could not be analysed, while others held to the view that the standard of taste was a rational and measurable phenomenon that could be scientifically determined. The philosopher David Hume (1711-76) championed the internalist cause, arguing that 'beauty is not a quality inherent in things: it exists only in the mind of the beholder', whereas his contemporary Immanuel Kant (1724-1802) maintained that aesthetic judgements had universal validity.

THE ONSLAUGHT OF MASS PRODUCTION

Neither of these two great minds could anticipate the explosive effect that the imminent industrial revolution was going to have upon taste. The era of mass production that the revolution begat was to turn all the social classes into consumers and bring the question of taste out of

The questionable sartorial mode and pompous demeanour of the dandies (above), who were prominent amongst the taste-makers of the early nineteenth century, underlines the fact that good taste is a purely subjective judgement. The Victorians favoured a high-minded but heavy-handed approach with the Great Exhibition (left), which the middle-classes were expected to attend and learn there what good taste was all about.

Henry Cole (top) was appalled at the thought that due to mass production, the world was becoming filled with objects that did not measure up to his own standards. Excess, however, was far from a uniquely British problem; this watercolour (above) was a design for a throne in Herrenchimsee Castle, in Germany.

the salons and on to the streets. Huge structural changes were forced on the economy and society of the time - as it shifted from a rural society to an industrial one - providing a more mobile, affluent and better-informed and educated populace. The peasants who augmented the workforce of the industrial revolution by settling in the towns as proletariat and petty bourgeois soon lost their contact with the folk culture of the countryside, and a new industrial culture based upon 'things' was waiting to be born.

By the start of the Victorian era there had been a sharp increase in public demand for goods and merchandise, fuelled by a vast expansion in the supply capacity, due to technological advances. Mass production made consumer goods available much further down the social scale than previously, a process which introduced variety into the question of taste as a single standard was no longer acceptable to the increased number and type of consumers. Although its champions fought a long rearguard action, taste was doomed as simply a highbrow issue concerned with rarified notions of art and of concern only to small coteries.

Many high-minded aesthetes found the produce of this new mass culture distasteful and were very concerned that the rapid changes in fashion and design were confusing the matter of taste. In Britain, where excesses of poor design were most apparent, Prince Albert, Henry Cole and a few other nobs considered it was important to teach an aesthetic sense to the middle classes who were buying all this stuff, and they set up the Great Exhibition of 1851 with this specific purpose in mind. Each specimen in the exhibition was 'selected for its merits in exemplifying some right principle of construction or ornament...to which it appeared desirable that the attention of our students and manufacturers should be directed', according to a publicity blurb at the time.

The exhibition was hugely successful, but did not have the didactic effect the good prince intended. It was reassembled a year later in Henry Cole's Museum of Manufactures at Marlborough House in Pall Mall. Cole decided to point up poor design in a much more direct way by setting up what he called the 'Chamber of Horrors' to display merchandise that offended his aesthetic sensibility. Cole and his colleagues were absolutely certain about what constituted false principles in design: lack of symmetry, disregard for structural form, formless confusion and concentration on the superficial aspects of design. However, their efforts were met with ridicule by a public that did not understand what they were going on about and needless to say

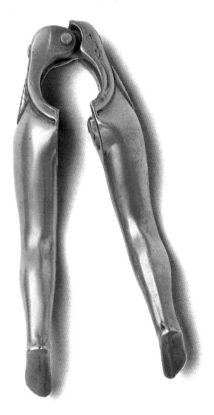

scarcely flattered manufacturers insisted on their wares being withdrawn; the Chamber of Horrors took an early bath.

To advocate the notion of good taste in this manner had, in fact, become a self-defeating exercise. As soon as there was a demand for objects which signified 'I have good taste' and these objects were mass-produced, then many people could possess them and claim the good-taste status the objects were supposed to bring. But this process of instant mass-acquisition and ownership of good taste meant the objects in question lost the element of exclusivity that formed a fundamental part of their appeal as symbols of good taste. Copying what was regarded as tasteful in the hope of being considered of good taste oneself created objects of no value because they were common. It also broke another rule of taste: having taste meant you exercised personal judgement in an enlightened way, but copying what other people had already approved removed this faculty of judgement almost entirely. This bourgeois bandwagonning, far from being the dawn of a glorious new age of universal discrimination, was to mark the origins of kitsch. It continues to this day - only now people try to gain their aesthetic brownie points by hanging a nastily framed reproduction Gainsborough or Turner on their chocolate painted artex walls.

This submarine fantasy is in fact a lamp, presumably for those who thought that the sea was a bright place. It is, naturally, the perfect memento from the south of France, where similar objects have been available since the forties.

Despite the attempts by various aesthetically philanthropic Victorians to impose good taste, there was little sign of improvement as the market for mass-produced goods spread down the social scale to the working classes. In the years between the Great Exhibition and the First World War the population of Western Europe and North America increased enormously. This expansion in population entailed changes in demography, in manufacturing and in distribution that created aesthetic ripples that Cole's Rules of Taste were only partially capable of containing.

A new breed of beings - professional art critics - came into existence with a special armory to assert their standards over what they saw as an aesthetic disaster. Above all, they needed a term to describe the worst manifestations of mass taste. The answer to their requirements lay in Viennese turn-of-the-century slang. The term 'verkitschen etwas' meant to knock off or cheapen something, and out of this was abstracted 'Kitsch'. Early critics pounced on the word to express their bitter contempt for many of the atrocities and hybrid expressions of taste that were beginning to appear in response to the surging demand for domestic goods. An Austrian art critic, Fritz Karpen, employed the term in his book of 1925, *Der Kitsch*, to describe certain unusual artefacts that bore designs that seemed crudely inappropriate and unnecessary to their purpose. Iron hooks containing poker-work of Leonardo Da Vinci's 'Last Supper' and inkwells manufactured in the shape of a female breast, featured memorably among the designs that he identified as devaluing the beauty of great art and the human form.

The term 'kitsch' itself had an extra dismissive power because it was specifically derived from a slang expression, which lent an added contempt to these feelings about the vulgarity of kitsch objects. But to some 'kitsch' did not cover merely the showily attractive. Some critics perceived kitsch as a far more insidious and far-reaching beast. Hermann Broch identified it not only with artistic wickedness but with social and political evil. In 1933 he commented: 'All periods in which values decline are kitsch periods. The last days of the Roman Empire produced kitsch and the present period [the era of the Third Reich]...cannot but be represented by aesthetic "evil" and the fear of evil and any art which is intended to express such an age adequately must also be an expression of the "evil" at work in it.' The author of the only other book on the topic, *Kitsch - An Anthology of Bad Taste* (published in 1968), Gillo Dorfles, saw the kitsch in Nazi art as residing in the bogus self-aggrandisement that is typical of fascism. This art had nothing to do with satisfying the tastes of the people; it was state art that produced meretricious images of muscular, heroic men and women or sentimental family groups for the people to admire and emulate.

In 1939 the art critic Clement Greenberg broadened the reference of the term and diluted some of the vitriol when he wrote that 'Kitsch is the culture of the masses'. For him, it was in fact the language through which the majority of people make sense of and give expression to their lives, and to Greenberg all popular artefacts were kitsch. With the steady growth of a popular culture since the early 1900s this analysis would mean that the entire century has been an endless spiral of cultural decline, (some defiant spirits may argue to the contrary).

For some time, the term kitsch remained in use purely for an appalled intelligentsia to disparage much of the produce of mass culture. After the cultural deep-freeze of the war years, the post-war public's appetites were hungry for change, diversity and opportunity. This pent-up energy exploded into life in the fifties with a new way of looking at the world and an enthusiastic optimism in the promise of 'the brave new world' of the future. Symbols of these new, bold and

The Draconian aesthetic principles of the Nazis provided the world with some of its most ponderous kitsch - confusing quasi-religious imagery with their own brutal ideology. The Aryan Frau by Liselotte Schramm is depicted as the Madonna with child (both with de rigueur blonde hair and blue eyes). The man-god born of the Fatherland, tutored in the Hitler youth, is, in the words of Richard Klein's title for his painting, Awakening to fulfil his noble destiny, complete with rather corporeal guardian angels.

Does this pretty letter rack with its three-dimensional depiction of Christ and the Disciples at the Last Supper really make a fitting reminder for tourists of why they came to London for their holidays?

exciting ideas were manifest in much of the art and design of the era and quickly became very popular. By the sixties, public taste was changing with increasing frequency, fuelled by a powerful and manipulative media, now augmented with the nuclear arsenal of television and a massive advertising industry. This cultural energy force carried itself to extremes during the 'swinging' decade.

It is said that art reflects society and the art of the sixties not only sought originality in the products of society but took up an extreme position that often appeared to pass the bounds of art. Art took imagery from elements of mass popular culture heretofore considered cheap and disposable - from soup cans and comic books to movie stars - and forced the issue of the kitsch of popular culture on to the intelligentsia's agenda. The concept of taste had come up for review but the population was now better educated and more opinionated than ever before and was not content to have their ideas of what was good or bad taste dictated by a wealthy elite. During the late sixties and the early seventies it was apparent to many people that there was actually something quite intriguing and even beautiful about what was previously disregarded as brash, gaudy and kitschy popular culture.

KITSCH COMES OF AGE

For a short while, in the late sixties and the early seventies, there was a widespread rejection of the whole idea of good taste and

14

consequently, there was no bad taste, but a massive celebration of any sort of culture from anywhere on the globe - literally anything went in any combination. In this great libertarian outburst inhibitions were eroded and barriers broken down; popular culture was recognised and celebrated as a creative manifestation of the spirit of freedom of expression of the time. The party did not last long (and looking at the platform shoes, perhaps it's just as well). During the course of the early part of the eighties, the issue of taste and all its incumbent problems of cultural status, snobbery and divisiveness began to slowly re-establish itself. This could perhaps be attributable to the first serious global economic crises for twenty years or so (1973-4 and 1979) and the political shifting to the right that occurred during the decade, with its speedy return to the comfort of traditional value systems. Or one could see it in terms of a cyclical theory which decrees that any trend is going to cause a reaction. In any event, almost invisibly it returned - but without toppling kitsch from its new status.

Taste is exercised on an exclusion and acceptance basis - by expressing your taste you are at once stating an allegiance to one aesthetic principle or other and a group of people who also share in your taste expression (e.g. pink champagne), whilst at the same time excluding yourself from competing taste preferences (e.g. canned lager). The cultural maelstrom that prevailed in the late sixties and early seventies had altered a number of peoples' views on the issue of taste. They learned that they could be less rigid in exercising their discrimination than before and it was acceptable to be more daring in expressing their taste - prime factors defining the course that kitsch would make to its current enormously popular status. Individuality and sophistication were the new goals to strive for in personal expression and it became cool to be able to dig anything you wanted - Beethoven, Jazz, the Beatles and New Wave music. The triumph of eclecticism and the consequent continuous and urgent search for new cultural delights made it possible for people actually to find a perverse pleasure in taste that had previously been regarded as simply awful. No stone would be left unturned in the quest for new tastes and styles. The new eclectic spirit meant that things that were previously perceived as other people's bad taste, such as china flying duck sets, could, if owned by somebody with a little more sophistication, be regarded as chic and witty. Despite the reassertion of the notions of good taste, a new beast emerged - people began to enjoy bad taste and the kitsch boom began.

During the seventies and eighties all kinds of products that had previously been considered as vile bad taste were quickly dusted down

During the sixties the Pop artists helped break the rules and boundaries in respect of art and taste. Warhol employed iconography drawn from the mass public's fascinations and obsessions - movie images, pop stars, comic books, even executions.

and reappraised as wonderfully funny and curious. There appeared books on trash movies, spoofs of trash movies, television re-runs of silly sit-coms, daft game shows inspired by daft game shows and television programmes anthologising mindless television programmes. What was actually happening was that by enjoying reruns of 'I Love Lucy' and 'Thunderbirds' people were excusing themselves for having laughed at them first time around. Bad taste was being enjoyed despite the promptings of your good angel to switch over and watch the documentary about the building of Victorian sewers. The cult of the trash aesthetic was also latched on to speedily by a public too young to remember the first showing of 'The Dick van Dyke Show', but which had been weaned on the commercialised post-war culture.

Kitsch has now outgrown its cult status and become a source for a great deal of comedy in mainstream cinema and on television, an issue of discourse in the fine arts and the basis for a moderate trade in second-hand furniture. A contemporary industry has emerged that deliberately produces objects and entertainments to be appreciated as kitsch, following the laws of supply and demand. The growing market of kitsch lovers want to spend their money on indulging their bad taste so things are now deliberately made to be perceived as kitsch. But this is a con and the punters are mistaken in believing that they are buying is real kitsch; what they are getting is bad taste inspired by it.

BAD TASTE WITH A DIFFERENCE

With this ambiguous response - you like what you know you're not supposed to like - kitsch has become a complex concept. Dictionaries define it either as 'worthless pretentiousness in the arts' - which simply identifies it with bad art - or as 'tawdry, vulgarised, popular art usually with sentimental appeal' - which identifies it with even worse art. Both definitions just relegate it to the confines of lower-class taste and well into the contempt zone. Neither definition gives you much idea of what it really might be, nor indeed do they recognise just how popular a consideration it has become. On the other hand, the current colloquial usage is generally too loose to be useful, as the word is often mis-applied now to anything that could be vaguely regarded as bad taste from the outrageously offensive to high camp.

Kitsch is somebody else's taste; to me it is in the way their misplaced idea of a good time clashes with mine. Like a warm pair of your big brother's flared trousers, after the initial shock subsides you can't help but enjoy it for what it really is: a darn good laugh. It is this wonder of what it was that made these things attractive to people

Instant kitsch. This little flower bloomed right at the end of the eighties to groove and bop along to all your favourite records.

These sickly sweet, gooey-eyed fluffinesses must originally have held an appeal to someone, somewhere, in order for them to have been designed, manufactured and purchased in the first place. The fascinating mystery as to whom precisely is a key factor in their appeal to kitsch fans the world over.

in the first place that is at the root of kitsch appeal. Kitsch is not simply bad taste, even though it is a creature of bad taste. It has a powerfully seductive ability both to attract and repel you at the same time. We have an almost childlike fascination with kitsch. Perhaps this is hardly surprising, with the gaudy, colourful, unusual shapes, the lack of sophistication and the nostalgic associations that much kitsch has. As it repels us by its clashes with our notions of good taste, it is this very awfulness that we find so appealing. Kitsch has to have the quality of excess: it has an energy that manifests itself in colour, decoration or sheer blatant tackiness that raises it above the merely bad.

The French poet Charles Baudelaire (1821-67) said, 'What is so intoxicating about bad taste is the aristocratic pleasure in being displeased.' The satisfying and exciting thing about liking things because 'they're so bad, they're good' is the brief but euphoric ego swell that occurs while being so aristocratically irked. A connoisseur of kitsch unconsciously applauds his or her own cleverness at being able to appreciate qualities inherent in objects that are undetectable to simpler folk. A feeling of superiority creeps over us, derived from the knowledge that some people genuinely draw comfort from these tasteless objects; this lofty delight is equal in importance to the kitsch lover as the physical tawdriness of the objects.

The reasons why things come to be regarded as kitsch start with the way that they clash with established notions of good taste. The more spectacular this collision, then the greater the resulting bad taste.

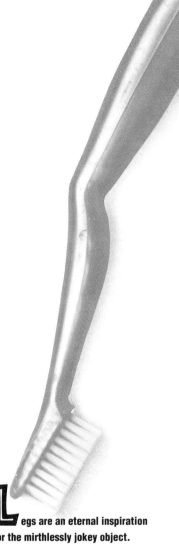

There is a sense of value integral to the idea that something is in good taste, a feeling of worth and importance. The kitsch item will firstly appear to devalue these notions, as happens when the image of the Mona Lisa appears on a tea-towel or keyring; kitsch remains faithful to its original meaning of 'to cheapen'. This does not mean that everything that is kitsch necessarily has actually to be cheap - a psychedelic paint job on a Rolls Royce or an over-ostentatious use of gold leaf on bathroom fittings can be considered as equally kitsch as a plastic ashtray proudly embossed with the image of the Turin Shroud. Both sets of examples are kitsch because they not only desecrate good taste icons, but they at once appear ugly and incomprehensible. To qualify as kitsch and not simply bad taste, there has to be a real sense of the ridiculous present. This ridiculousness manifests itself in many ways. It could be in the sheer inappropriateness of stubbing out your cigarette on a plastic rendition of a religious icon, or in the pretentiousness of having gold on a functional object like bathroom taps, or in the ostentatious display of a supposedly alternative lifestyle on a prestige car like a Rolls Royce.

Just as refinement and dignity are integral to good taste, so excess and impropriety are innate properties of kitsch. There is an inane and comic crudity present in green, penis-shaped candles or garish pink toothbrushes moulded as shapely female legs that compels kitsch lovers to go out and buy them.

Kitsch wouldn't exist were it not for the public's fickle quest for satiety, propelled by the commercial pressures of advertising, the media and social status. Our culture produces a vast amount of objects which

Legs are an eternal inspiration for the mirthlessly jokey object. Nodding dogs, however, came and fortunately went from the back shelf of cars, but are now much sought after by collectors.

are sought after, acquired and finally discarded by society as public taste constantly moves on in search of new ideas and styles. Without this wasteful aspect of our economic system there would be no kitsch - and what a shame that would be. The modern kitsch lover is a true 'green', a cultural recycler - he looks through the great proliferation of schlock and rescues from it what makes him laugh, then throws a rude gesture at the idea of 'good taste' and all the social rules and codes that we are supposed to abide by.

The purpose of this book is to get you over your inhibitions and into sync with kitsch, whether you're already an ardent collector of aristocratic displeasures or suspicious of the trash culture. During this study, we shall journey through the entire perverted phenomenon of bad taste, often taking obtuse and tangential diversions made to help trace a route through to the true centre of kitsch. Our aim is to better understand, appreciate and hopefully learn to love this gloriously inverted form of snobbery. Welcome to the awful things in life in all their lurid glory - after all, they are all around us now, be it your tie, shoes or hairstyle, on the cover of that magazine over there or that junk shop sofa that you're sitting on watching some trashy TV programme. Don't forget to bring your sense of humour along - enjoy the good clean fun of the kitsch phenomenon.

Holiday postcards are bought at your weakest moment - the value of money seems insignificant in the two-week-long attempt to relax and have fun, and the brain is well addled from too much sun, beer and other people. Postcard manufacturers have never shown any crusading zeal for restimulating the higher thought processes.

IN EVERY DREAM HOME A HEARTACHE

Imagine this scenario. You're visiting somebody's home for the first time ever and they get called out of the house for some reason - the cat's been run over, say, or the next door neighbour's locked himself out again and needs to borrow a ladder to regain entry. You're on your own in their front room for a full five minutes. For the student of taste this is a perfect moment. In this short time you can learn more about your next door neighbour, potential lover or dentist than hours of conversation, eating or drinking together will ever tell you. You have the key to unlock their tastes, their hopes, their neuroses even.

Go on, have a little browse along the mantelpiece, the shelves, the walls and if you can manage it, make a quick foray into a drawer or two. For it is all here, in the living room, kitchen, boudoir and bathroom, the stuff that we are really made of. It is at home that people commit themselves to the most intensively personal and revealing manifestations of their taste. What a person may choose to wear for work or to a nightclub often carries very few clues to their real selves. You can discard an ill-fitting and unfashionable work uniform at the end of a sweaty day's toil and metamorphose from a sensible bank clerk into a wild disco king for the weekend, but you can't change your wallpaper just for a dinner party.

Even if you fail to unearth a vast treasure of revelatory objets d'art amongst the chattels and effects during your five minutes alone in your neighbour's house, so widespread has the trash ethos become now that it is likely that at the very least there will be a little island of kitsch floating in a sea of conventional 'good' taste. It could be that tomato shaped ketchup pot stolen from a burger bar nestling next to

It's twee time! The eighties saw a vogue for making objects in the shape of others that were functionally quite different, but as this pre-war timepiece testifies, such ideas were far from new.

the windmill cruet set, or the knitted doll toilet roll cover. No matter how small or how well tucked away, you will find them, unadulterated and vital clues to what people are really about.

YESTERDAY'S FUTURE TODAY

Although kitsch itself has a long and venerable past, much of what is instantly identified as kitsch today dates from that celebrated decade of design excess - the fifties. Although probably the first common household object to be widely reappropriated as kitsch were flying duck sets which date from the thirties, it is the lamps, coffee tables, armchairs and sofas, dining tables, TV sets, rugs, curtains, blinds, linoleum, carpets, crockery, cutlery, tableware, glassware, wallpaper, fabrics, ashtrays and ornaments of the fifties which provide the largest store of materials for the kitsch collector. They are still (relatively) abundant, and, by golly, they're noticeable.

The designs of the fifties differed greatly from the ordered symmetry of the austere post-war era. Fifties designers were inspired by science - molecules, atoms, spaceships, kidneys and boomerangs (boomerangs?). These themes were manifested in the asymmetrical shapes of everything they designed from furniture to tableware.

The fifties saw a radical stylistic departure from the war-dominated home furnishings of the previous decade. The whole world appeared to explode into colour and a whole variety of new and different shapes and combinations materialised. No longer were there only browns, greens, dark blues, maroons, blacks and whites but an entire palette of hues from which to paint the new world - pastel pinks, yellows, greens, lilacs, blues and oranges, violet, cerise, magenta, gold, lime green or turquoise. All these colours quickly became incredibly fashionable and never mind if they didn't particularly go together. Home furnishings were now bright, vivid and bold rather like the advertising of the era.

Once unleashed, the shapes of things went wild too, and lost the symmetry that the old, ordered world insisted upon. Fifties design either had or gave the illusion of asymmetrical irregularity, with inventive and wide ranging reference sources. Molecular structures, amoebas, kidneys and boomerangs appeared in the shapes of all kinds of domestic goods from coffee tables to ashtrays. There were bold new patterns too - chevrons, zebra stripes, leopard spots, polka dots, leaves and abstract jumbles that could have come from surrealist paintings took over wallpaper patterns and upholstery fabrics.

The designers and manufacturers of the fifties saw their job as filling the drab and dull functional voids that had been the interiors of most peoples' homes for the previous 15 years. What they were giving a generation that for the first time had some spare cash to spend was a bewildering array of alien furniture, shapes and colours. An element of 'other worldliness' dominated design, representing the most exciting

Through the expanding media, the world was shrinking daily in the fifties - a phenomenon that was reflected in a taste for exotica. It was utterly and indiscriminately patronising: Chinamen, Red Indians and Negresses decorated all kinds of domestic hardware from salt and pepper shakers to teapots.

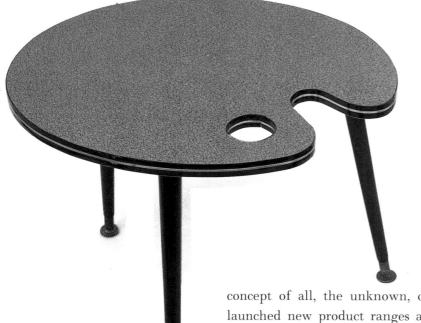

concept of all, the unknown, or the future. Marketing men regularly launched new product ranges as 'shapes of things to come'. There was a childlike fascination with the possibilities of the future, and with space travel, prompted by advances in science and the development of real, visible space programmes.

The designers and manufacturers of the fifties used the materials and the technology that helped them win the war in a less destructive but in no less an aggressive fashion. The mass production of plastic goods had been perfected and a comprehensive range of products that were cheaper to produce and distribute than ever before could now be made for the home. This meant that people could acquire almost any object that they wanted for the home at a fraction of the cost that it would have been before. To oil the wheels of the post-war economic boom the money to buy these things became easier to come by. A proliferation of money lending schemes sprang up, especially 'hire-purchase'. In terms of taste this was all very significant. Instead of having to wait ten years while you saved to buy a new leather Chesterfield, you could now go out and get yourself a brand new blue vinyl three piece suite at a third of the price and ten per cent down.

For many people it was also the first time that they could afford to buy significant numbers of non-functioning objects to decorate their mantelpiece and walls. Plaster-cast depictions of anything from the natural world, from fruit to animals to human beings themselves sprouted upon lounge walls everywhere. Swans, ducks (of course), flamingoes, leopards, cheetahs and panthers brought a touch of exotica to peoples' lives in a world that appeared to be shrinking daily through the growing media. Little plaster depictions of Chinamen, Mexicans

24

Shape was matched by colour. There was an entire new palette in which to depict the consumer paradise - pastels, violet, cerise, magenta, lime green and turquoise replaced the drab colours of the previous two decades.

and Negroes gathered on mantelpieces and on top of the new electric fires. These cute and friendly creatures were so obliging they would often allow you to stub your cigarette out on their little smiling faces.

THE SEVENTIES AND BEYOND

The true kitsch connoisseur possesses a keen appreciation of slightly bizarre, atypical ornamental and furniture objects from any decade. But the objects he delights in have not all had to wait as long as 30-40 years to move from contemptible kitsch to collectable kitsch. The wax bubble lamps, optical fibre sculptures and executive toys that were popular in the seventies and the see-through inflatable armchairs of

In the design ethos of the fifties the world outside of Manchester and Philadelphia was a funny, cute place. The exotic started with Caribbean women and ended with tomatoes. No wonder the ducks, by now a staple feature of the Modern Home, wanted to migrate.

26

HINE
SIGNATURE
Fine Cognac
★ ★ ★

Turn on, tune in and gloop out. The lava-lamp gave psychedelia to seventies suburbia without the hassle of drugs. Production ceased when fashion turned instead to Mickey Mouse telephones, not, as a popular myth had it, because they gave off dangerous fumes. But the revivalist cult is now proving so popular that the original manufacturers have resumed production. Business is booming.

the late sixties all now appeal to the trash sense of humour. Like much kitsch, it now seems incomprehensible that objects such as these could have been once greatly admired and fashionable. Likewise, lowbrow art can send the kitsch collector into paroxysms of pleasure. Posters that sold in enormous quantities during the seventies in stores such as Athena and Hallmark like the one of the female tennis player who forgot her knickers, 'pussyfoot' and a windswept Farrah Fawcett-Majors have now made their debut appearances on the walls of kitsch avant-gardists.

DULLSVILLE

From the time they first hit the shops these domestic goods were recognised as kitsch by the tastemakers, who regarded them all as examples of vulgar working-class taste. The cheap materials, vivid colours and crass depictions of people, plants and animals horrified them and make us laugh today for the same reason: because they conflict with the values of good taste.

We, of course, can afford to be amused. Take, for instance, the fifties. We live in that future world that so interested them, and we know it better. We can accordingly giggle at their naive misconceptions and maybe we are also comforted by the cosy nostalgic route they offer

28

from the realities of that future. But there are other reasons why we embrace the fifties' gaudiness. We purport to like our houses to have traditional rural themes, shapes and colours. We like plain all-wool carpets in our living rooms, flagstone floors in our hallways and real wood if we can afford it in our kitchens, and we generally place great store in the use of time-honoured, long-lasting materials such as timber, iron and brick. And yet we will place on the pine dresser a lamp with cocktail-stick-and cherry legs and a lemon-yellow plastic shade decorated with black amoebas. It makes you think, doesn't it?

We love our plaster-cast pink flamingoes and Negroid ashtrays not just because we are consenting adults and in private we like to practise inverted snobbery, but also because when it comes to what has been available to fill our houses, flats and bedsits we have been deprived of fun for ten years. In the eighties one colour was allowed, Henry Ford-style, for the smart objects we brought into our homes - black (we were probably wearing black when we bought them in, too). The bland dogmatism of the matt-black eighties really was like an endurance test; this was Dullsville, Arizona. But how much blandness can you take? At one point in mid-decade it seemed as if all objects were available in silhouette only. Who really needs a matt-black egg cup, for God's sake?

The matt-black ethos was a form of cultural fascism - forcing the consumer on to a track towards very narrow and specific expressions of taste that were almost utterly foolproof. The 'tasteful' consumer had no choice available, except for shape and dimension. Matt-black was the culmination of a long process of reductionism in design by which any feature not considered as essential to the function of an object was jettisoned from the drawing board towards the wastepaper basket. It all began with the Bauhaus school of design in the 1920s, and we know where that led to in architecture - to unlamented tower blocks on windy inhuman estates. We all know, don't we?, that the ultimate aim of the perpetration of these structures was to destroy the importance of the individual in society and to force people to function collectively, with no quirkiness or eccentricity or fun whatsoever.

Yet so many people of impeccable taste have willingly submitted to this ethos when it comes to buying alarm clocks, hi-fis, TVs and video equipment. It's not surprising that we've sneaked out to the market and bought some bright and bouncy fifties objet. But it's only a joke, of course, our real taste is slim and black. But maybe in the end the matt-black will be seen as another form of futurism like the stuff from the fifties, and by the year 2000 your matt black Walkman will be kitsch. Who knows?

Well blow me! This incredibly sexist and racist ashtray from the fifties proves that the matt black ethic needn't only be concerned with dull minimalist conformity.

GOD AND MONA LISA

If we commit the crime of taking God's name and using it in vain, either speaking in profanities or in conjunction with naughty swearwords, we can be accused of blasphemy. But what is it when an image of God, the Virgin Mary or Jesus Christ, or a depiction of a Biblical scene, is reproduced as part of a low-grade plastic holy water holder? Yes, it's kitsch, and when it is nailed to the hall wall of an agnostic TV executive's pad in Hampstead or SoHo, it's clever and you've won the purple padded ashtray on a stand.

Three-dimensional depictions of religious figures and scenes manufactured in cheap, tacky materials are in evidence all over the kitsch-conscious world. A plastic bedside lampbase depicting the Stations of the Cross provides us with an opportunity to laugh at its bogus pomp and piousness and the utter inappropriateness of the application. But then most of this sort of kitsch paraphernalia is sold by the churches themselves. I often wonder if they are in on the joke too.

Tawdry crucifixions and lachrimose weeping Virgins manifest an extreme form of kitsch - the high seriousness of religion reduced to empty sentimental expressions in the name of popularisation. The kitsch that dwells within these bastard interpretations of holy images is also evident in the other area of life associated with seriousness and profundity, High Art. There can be few other images other than that of God in his various forms that carry as much cultural value as that of

Does God get a percentage of the takings from his merchandise? Such pieces of religious ephemera are available in cathedral shops the world over. It makes you wonder if the church is in on the joke too.

the Mona Lisa. If you asked any member of the public what the best-known painting in the world is, you can bet your bottom Deutschmark that Leonardo Da Vinci's surprisingly small depiction of a half-smiling, plain, unknown lady ranks way up there in the top three. Somehow, this frankly boringly static and murky oil painting has become a symbol of greatness in conventional art. Its high status in Western culture has led to the same seemingly criminal reproduction ad illegitimentum. It is not only near the Louvre in Gai Paris that this winsome individual's fizzog is available on everything from spectacle cases to tea towels, but she has sold her image to act as a trademark on a whole array of odd produce from fabrics purporting to be 100% Nylon 'Horsehair' (Duralon) to red wine!

It's worth keeping your eyes open when you're on your travels for bastardised High Art - it can make the most witty household

The high cultural (and copyright free) status of such images as the Mona Lisa and Roman and Greek statuary has led to the reproduction of their likenesses ad infinitum on the most unlikely and inappropriate objects.

accoutrement and you'll surely be rewarded with polite applause from fellow kitsch freaks. Michelangelo's David is available in all sorts of tacky forms, but the best example I've come across is a reproduction as a candle with grotesquely enlarged genitalia in a porn shop in Amsterdam. If this appears a little too strong, there are all sorts of old masters available at local department stores in suitably cheap gold-painted plastic frames. Why, you could make your own hallway just like a top art gallery with a Haywain, a Laughing Cavalier, Whistler's 'Mother', and as a final touch, a small Venus de Milo statuette with tasteful garden fountain effect.

THE GREATEST ARTIST IN THE WORLD

For most people the act of hanging a particular picture on a wall at home serves two functions - one simply as decoration (not everyone likes to be surrounded by large expanses of blank emulsion) and the other to make some sort of statement about themselves and about where they stand in the world in terms of taste and status. Enter a Russian-born South African, who became one of the biggest-selling artists the world has ever seen. You'll recognise his work instantly but despite his monolithic success you probably won't know his name. It's Vladimir Tretchikoff.

Some artists dispose of their work through the medium of art galleries and agents and some travel the land, setting up their easels and their camps at likely spots and selling their canvases as souvenir views of the surrounding landscape. But the biggest market for the popular painter is in published reproductions. The best selling portfolio in the world between 1950-62 came from the brush of Tretchikoff. His portraits of African, Asian and Oriental subjects such as Zulus, African warriors and tribespeople and the ordinary working blacks of Southern Africa like flower sellers, fishermen and herb-sellers sprouted upon parlour walls the world over for a decade or more. Probably his most famous were his 'Green Lady' series.

His depictions of these simple folk epitomised the most typical characteristics of populist art through the ages - sentimental allusions, popular subject matter, blatant colours, and a sum of technical effects. The public loved Tretchi's pictures because they brought a touch of the exotic into their front room and they were portraits of human beings that they could understand and weren't like the weird abstract art that was big at the time. The characters stared out at you in an almost mystical, inquisitive manner, and above all else they were colourful, pretty images that made the front room feel lived in. Ordinary people felt comfortable with Tretchikoff, and they could afford him.

Although Trechi exhibited in galleries around the world and the crowds flocked to the openings of these events literally in their thousands, more significantly, he also held exhibitions in department stores. You could view the original in oils there first and then buy a reproduction for just a few modest dollars, including the frame!

However, despite his enormous success (and vast personal profit), he has been not so much reviled as simply ignored by the official art world. There are few references to him in any art compendiums, text-books or reviews of the time, yet he was enormously popular all over the world. Tretchi committed the cardinal sin of commercialising his work and selling it to the masses. He was happy to hang on the hall walls of Surbiton rather than some chi-chi boho artspot in Greenwich Village and that gets stuck right up the skyward-pointing noses of the art mafiosi.

Tretchikoff today is not to be found on suburban walls, his work having gone out of style. In the comparative safety of the pitched roofs and neo-Georgian leaded window aesthetics, today an ordinary person's reaction to a Tretchi would probably be initially one of laughter and then recollection that their grannie used to have this sort of stuff hanging above the mantelpiece. But to the kitsch enthusiast the combination of the incredible low cost, their 'common' place in the world, the impossibly clear complexions lit from above by an eerie, even alien green light, mixed with exotic costumes depicted in the familiar vivid kitsch colours of pink, purple, cerise, lime green, magenta and turquoise, the stilted, unnatural poses and the weird over-your-shoulder direction of the subjects' gaze provide an irresistible and deeply loved item of bad taste for bedrooms, lounges and toilets.

If the idea of placing an ad in the 'goods wanted' column of *The Times* for mint-condition Tretchikoffs seems a bit of an expensive and time-consuming effort just to acquire a little bit of kitsch, you can of course pick it up easily from Tretchi's heirs with any of the stuff you see hanging up on park railings or in open-air markets in the world's major cities on a Sunday afternoon. This stuff is truly, truly amazing - not because it represents any astounding advances in the science of trash aesthetics but because the pictures are just so unbelievably awful. Endless autumnal landscapes, horses galloping in the sea and nude nymphets rising in vacuum-formed plastic from a canvas of several hues of the same subtly airbrushed abstracted background are very definitely not the produce of sound human minds. But, nevertheless, these artists come, go and sell these strange interpretations of life quite respectably each Sunday. The only rational explanation is that at the end of the day they go back to Mars in their spaceships that look remarkably like half-restored Morris Travellers or ancient Chevvies. And when these pictures finally make it to a lounge wall somewhere in Tokyo, Des Moines or Croydon the Martians tune in and can see through the pictures and into the living rooms to study this strange species that actually seems to like the things.

DESIGNER KITSCH AND SOUVENIR STANDS

For many people, the art of the park railings is in the vanguard of kitsch. It's not tried and tested foolproof stuff, proven by time and rendered acceptable by the softening blur of nostalgia. It's contemporary, and you have to be bold to buy it. After all an observer might take this as being your real taste. What a ghastly idea!

But, of course, those in the right circles know that, as a person of discrimination, you could only have bought this stuff with your tongue in your cheek. However, there is a seductive array of far less obvious contemporary goods, waiting to trap the unwary. Perhaps if you are seen with one of these you might get the Flying Duck Award after all.

In the late seventies and the early eighties a new sort of kitsch came to be. It was especially manufactured for those possessed of a once-safe sensibility. Freshly minted, clean and therefore somewhat sanitised, 'safe' kitsch became available in gift shops, novelty shops and

The great Vladimir Tretchikoff unfortunately declined our invitation to have his art appear in this book. All the same, his influence, like his fortune, has been immense. The two French artists/designers Pierre et Gilles produced their 'Medusa' as a eulogy to his unmistakeable style.

34

Mementoes of holidays. The Leaning Tower of Pisa was probably made in Hong Kong, and the snowstorm paperweights were almost certainly so - most are. Snowstorms are popular collectors items: they are cheap to acquire, attractive to look at, and can bring back wonderful memories of many a happy holiday spent, say, in the snows of Florida or the Costa Brava. They also brighten up any bathroom.

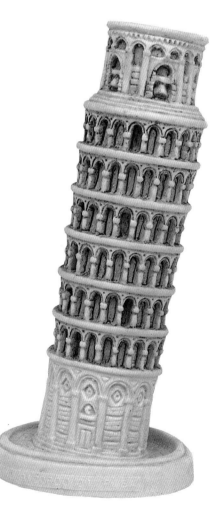

those establishments that tend to call themselves 'general stores'. And it was sold and still is - right up there on the shelves beside the 'good' taste. Terracotta and French farmhouse bakeware finds itself alongside fruit and vegetable-shaped crockery, while neat German china suffers the indignity of being placed next to teapots depicting opera singers or with ballet dancer's legs, 'celebrity' teacups and joke garden ornaments. Woe betide the hand that strays a bit too far to one side.

Do I hear you muttering, 'But these thing aren't kitsch, just rather fun - and quite clever really'? Well next time you're shopping for a present or have a few minutes to while away, and are tempted into one of these glittering emporiums in some shopping mall fashioned out of a resurrected warehouse or defunct nineteenth-century market, just stand back for a moment. Instead of plunging in, have a good look at it. Despite the smattering of good taste, is there anything of real lasting value in the rest? Doesn't the whole place look little more than a sort of upmarket souvenir stall? Go on, be honest!

Admit this comparison, and it is the kiss of death. For it is at souvenir stalls that you will find the anorak-brigade of kitsch enthusiasts most in their element. It is at these tacky little kiosks that stand on smoggy street corners of busy city thoroughfares and beach boulevards throughout the world that modern kitsch is most easily recognisable, in worthless little knick-knacks that however cheap are never worth what you pay for them. The classic kitsch of snowstorm paperweights, metallic-lettered or souvenir-view ashtrays, naked lady pens, illuminated miniatures of famous buildings or national monuments cling to these stalls like the pigeons on the city's buildings.

But while these are easy to spot, kitsch changes with the same speed as its brother, fashion. Ever-new forms are always being produced to catch out those who let their guard slip for a moment. If you are not careful you can easily plunge into a personal relationship with an object that will have those wiser fellows who will follow us asking, open mouthed, 'But how could anyone ever have bought that stuff seriously?'

Advice to collectors: the souvenir stands that populate street corners at tourist destinations the world over are a good, inexpensive place to start to your own little kitsch treasury.

TINSELTOWN, TURKEYS AND TEENAGERS

THE DREAM FACTORY

The story of kitsch in the cinema begins and ends with Hollywood, the centre of film production in the world for the past 80 years or so. Its influence upon Western culture cannot be underestimated. We all know that the saccharin-sweet dream world of Hollywood cinema is an unattainable reality, but every time we submit to watching a mainstream commercial film produced, financed or just distributed from that small suburb north-west of Los Angeles, we never fail to suspend our disbelief. Somehow we need to believe in our dreams, albeit temporarily.

Behind the glossy fiction of the silver screen, the kitsch of Hollywood is clearly evident. It is to be found in the false sentiment and the phony characters, the plucking at the heart-strings, the unreal dialogue, sweetly happy endings, bogusly wholesome standards and ham-fisted moralising. The system itself could have been designed as a machine for producing kitsch, with conceited and avaricious stars whose mollycoddled infantile demands were for a long time sustained by a star system that cosseted them from reality. The system itself has been oiled by money, the great driving force behind its professed virtuousness; its orders have been given by cynical producers demanding effects and plots that will hit the public at its weakest point, while themselves finding time for the occasional tear prompted by some shallow effect that appeals to their own mawkish sensibilities. Sure there have been some great movies, but think of the quality

Carmen Miranda (left) showing that Hollywood knows how to go bananas about style in the 1943 musical, *The Gang's All Here* (released as *The Girls He Left Behind* in the UK). Low budget movies (above) achieve a less glossy but often more quirky tackiness.

39

(never mind the length) of some of the biggest hits. Who could sit through *The Sound of Music* twice, let alone 367 times, without needing hospital treatment for a laughter-induced hernia?

There is a further kitsch twist in the hypocrisy of the whiter-than-white public image that the movie world promotes of itself. This is aided and abetted by a public which both both avidly believes the grand facade and equally reveres the scandals and disgraces which have plagued Hollywood since the twenties (see Kenneth Anger's two *Hollywood Babylon* volumes). But let's not become too pious about this issue. If we are honest with ourselves, the debasing amount of power heaped upon these mere mortals' shoulders by fame, money and public attention are bound to make corruption and vice natural by-products.

KITSCH ON A LOW BUDGET

The shortcomings of mainstream Hollywood, the A-movies, have been enough written about to need no addition here. Anyway, these are not the films that appeal to the real kitsch aficionado. For one thing, they provide none of the thrill of discovery, and for another, when you're seen coming out of *Mary Poppins* with traces of popcorn around your mouth, how does anyone know that you didn't go just because you think it's good clean family entertainment?

Regular movies are multi-million dollar operations in which no one person rarely has a free rein - unless they're Steven Spielberg or Clint Eastwood, of course. However, most movies that are made on a low budget are transcendent expressions of a single person's quirky originality, and this gives them a special quality. The movies that are the most fun and simultaneously the most kitsch are to be found in this low-budget tradition.

The B-movie was a child born of the Depression. Between 1930 and 1933 cinema attendances in the USA fell drastically from around 90 million per week to nearer 60 million. Work and money being increasingly harder to find meant that the customary fare of a single feature film supported by cartoons and shorts was beginning to lose its appeal to the public. The solution was found in the double bill, which offered the public two or three hours of entertainment at the same price. This seemed a real bargain to the audiences of the Depression, despite the glaring fact that the second film was an inferior low-budget quickie. It would feature not stars but instead those actors in town who could fit the clothes that the studio's wardrobe department had available at the time.

The potential for kitsch was huge, albeit for opposite reasons from

It was a great day for budget-conscious B movie makers when they discovered that songs were a cheaper way of rolling back the Red Indians than expensive cavalry and bullets. Gene Autrey first hit the big time on a radio programme called 'The Oklahoma Yodeling Cowboy'. Enough said.

Keep your hands off my chemistry set! Flash Gordon belonged to an era of heroes when smart bombs were those that sat around waiting long enough for you to defuse them before they went off. (Below) Johnny Sheffield as Bomba, the Jungle Boy in one of a series of movies knocked out in the late forties that capitalised on the Tarzan boom. Making cheap imitations of successful originals has become entrenched behaviour for the movie industry, and has provided a ready-made vehicle for more recent, deliberately kitsch directors.

those of the over-inflated big-budget numbers. Most of the B-movies were made with the offcuts of the A-movie productions and at a fraction of the cost and time. These shortcomings provided a challenge to the B-movie-makers since the same locations and script material were deployed from one film to another, so a considerable amount of ingenuity was required on the part of the filmmaker to avoid a strong sense of déjà-vu being invoked in the audiences' minds. The B-movies were the youth training scheme for new talent, with both directors and stars cutting their teeth on these low-budget flicks. Such Hollywood luminaries as William Wyler, Fred Zinnemann, Lana Turner, Ava Gardner and Glenn Ford all learned their trade in them.

The sub-genre provides an appreciable source of mildly kitschy thrills. Most of Ronald Reagan's acting career, especially in *Bedtime for Bonzo* (in which he co-starred with a chimpanzee), comes into this category, as do the science fiction B-movie serials of *Flash Gordon* and *Buck Rogers*, with their rickety space ships and costumes that appear as if torn from the backs of extras from *The Wizard of Oz* and *Robin Hood*. Sub-Tarzan films like *Bomba, the Jungle Boy* flocked out of the jungle following the success of the originals. They fought for space with the countless B-westerns, particularly those featuring crooning cowboys such as Tex Ritter and Gene Autrey (*Mystery Mountain* and *Steel Faces*).

Bedtime for Bonzo is wonderfully ludicrous. Nobody should miss the President-to-be in a story based on the premise that 'even a monkey brought up in the right surroundings can learn the meaning of decency'. A chimpanzee called Bonzo pulls off a jewellery robbery and his scientist-trainer (Reagan) naturally gets the blame. Amazingly, Reagan refused the sequel as he felt the story wasn't strong enough!

Bomba, the Jungle Boy was the first in a series of 12 quickie-features, capitalising on the Tarzan craze. Ironically, Bomba was played by an 18-year-old, Johnny Sheffield, who himself had been sacked from the Tarzan series for being overweight. The budgets were so tight that footage from a 1930 documentary, *Africa Speaks*, was used for jungle exteriors for all 12 pictures.

What tinges these B-movies with their kitsch appeal is their relationship with mainstream Hollywood. Produced with hand-me-down sets and spare wardrobe and studio time, the B-flicks always fitted neatly in the Hollywood genres of western, musical, thriller, etc. However, they all lacked the very ingredients that were vital to Big Brother's films such as high-quality production values and stars. For all this the B-movies were the luxury end of the low-budget movie

Well, which would you rather share your bed with? B-movie megastar, president-to-be Ronald Reagan clearly doesn't mind that Diana Lynn ends up with chimpanzee Bonzo in *Bedtime for Bonzo* (1951). Soon after this jolly chronicle of simian misadventures was released, its screenwriter was labelled a Communist and never wrote another movie.

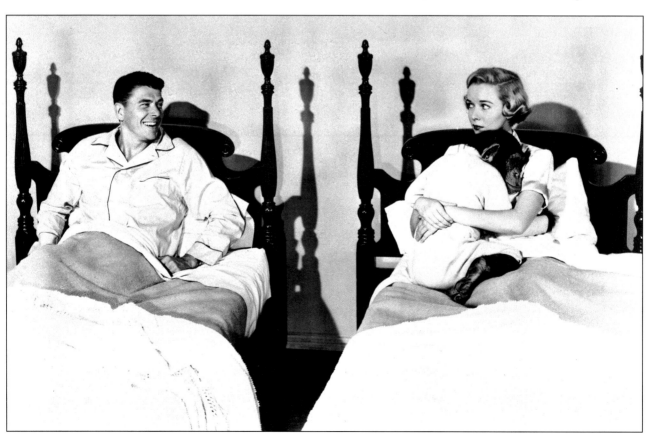

industry and are only the starting point. The real fun begins further down the financial scale.

YOUTH EXPLOITATION MOVIES

We've heard the term (haven't we?), but, well, what exactly is an exploitation movie? Well, it's a term given to a B-movie that's tailor-made for a specific audience by playing upon its known interest in a particular subject, supposedly in the name of social concern, but in reality in order to entertain. Kitsch movie lovers please take note.

For example, the first films that could be considered 'exploitation' appeared in the very early days of the cinema, and featured taboo themes and popular scandals. They had tell-all titles like *Gambling Exposed* and *The Curse of the Drink*. By the mid-forties movie makers began to wake up to youth as a market force. The happy-go-lucky kids portrayed by Judy Garland and Mickey Rooney in Hollywood - themselves pretty sickly-sweet to modern eyes - had darker siblings in the shape of juvenile delinquents. It was known that they were a popular subject from the pulp books and magazines that featured them.

The first independent producer really to define exploitation was a peculiarly-named former journalist and ad man, Kroger Babb. His headline-inspired quickies of the late forties and early fifties included an unwanted pregnancy flick, *She Shoulda Said No*, which was screened at late-night adults-only shows, and an anti-marijuana film, *The Devil's Weed*. The latter starred Lila Leeds, an actress who had been busted with Robert Mitchum for possession of the evil herb .

Babb's real talent was in discovering markets the major studios barely bothered with: small towns where local cinemas either couldn't make much profit from the high-rental major productions, or where there were no cinemas at all. Babb would either rent a local hall and bring in his projector or, failing that, would set up a marquee that he carried around in a truck. He was a brilliant salesman whose gimmicks would inspire future exploitationists. The most audacious of these were to segregate the audiences by sex for 'hot' flicks and to have a nurse in attendance for shockers. He also offered prizes and giveaways.

Arguments raged about whether these films had an adverse effect on the public psyche. On the one hand, it was said that by demonstrating these evils, then people may be less likely to fall prey to them, but on the other hand there was the more plausible theory that motion picture producers were merely providing salacious thrills. This heady confusion of morality and base human demand for vice provided the perfect chemical mixture for kitsch cinema.

The first 'exploitation' films of the early fifties were concerned with taboo themes and popular scandals - such as juvenile delinquency and prostitution. They had titles that promised experiences far more exciting than those the actual movies ever delivered.

In reality the only effect they were likely to have on any psyche was stultification. Billed as 'the world's first educational sex-hygiene film' *Mom and Dad* is disappointingly only a moralistic love story. *The Devil's Weed* is a sort of National Enquirer kiss-and-tell exposé, lacking the power of another exploitation film that deals with drugs, *Reefer Madness*, in which one puff of pot leads clean-cut teenagers down the road to insanity and death.

Three events precipitated the growth of exploitation cinema in America. The first occurred in 1953 when the Anti-Trust laws were devised to bust up monopolies. This divorced the exhibition and distribution ends of the movie business from the production end. Coincidentally, audiences were once again on a downward slippery slope from a post-war peak of 100 million admissions per week to the 40 million reached in 1957.

Secondly, the rise in the popularity of television - sales of TV sets reached 20,000 daily in 1956 - was having a pronounced effect on audiences' expectations. Unlike the cinema-goers of the thirties, they didn't want more, they wanted better. Television had taken over the function of showing the B-movie. If you could watch a mediocre western on TV for nothing, why pay to see one at the cinema?

The movie business was running scared. It tried to fight back with various inane gimmicks that produced their own kitsch products. Sensurround, Hallucinogenic Hypnovision, Percepto, Psychorama and others attempted to extend the cinematic experience into a third dimension - the Hollywood dreams were now physically trying to reach out to touch the audience. But these bizarre inventions all too often only provided audiences with unpleasant experiences that had them running back to the safety zone of the front room and the small square box within moments of the film starting. Some progress.

Smell-O-Vision, for example, was developed by Liz Taylor's stepson, Mike Todd Jr, for *The Scent of Mystery* (1960), which starred Denholm Elliott and Peter Lorre. During the course of the movie up to 50 dubiously artificial essences could be pumped out into the auditorium, controlled by the film's synchronised 'smell track'. Among the fragrances used were roses, peaches, wood shavings, ocean breeze, oil paint, garlic and gunsmoke. Homage was paid to this device some years later by John Waters in his kitsch classic, *Polyester*, which was screened with scratch'n'sniff cards handed to the audience. Waters named his technological advance 'Odorama', but this time the scents included recently vacated car seat leather, trash cans, pizzas and, somewhat inevitably, a fart.

44

The third and perhaps most fundamental factor in the evolution of the trashy exploitation movie was the emergence in the fifties of a clearly identifiable new creature - the Teenager. Previously there had only been children and adults, with a brief period of awkward adolescence in between, and nobody made movies for adolescents. What for? They had no money, and anyway, they were here today and gone tomorrow. But teenagers were a different matter entirely. They emerged fully developed at 13, lined their pockets by babysitting and washing cars and were still around six years later. They became an economic power in themselves; they provided a vitally important new market for all kinds of products from hamburgers to soda pop and blue jeans to Elvis Presley. They also wanted their own films.

This was the era of the drive-in cinema, when the automobile was king in post-war boom town America and the kids acting like grown-ups were getting younger and younger every day. The exploitation films they liked were not shown as B-pictures, they were double-billed, pretending to be two main features. If they were successful enough first time around, they were dusted off later on and sent in support of a newer movie. The major studios were left floundering in the wake of companies like Hallmark (owned by Babb) and Monogram, but would not stoop to the kids' taste for the sensational, gruesome or suggestive. This was tough luck for the majors as they were losing out to the

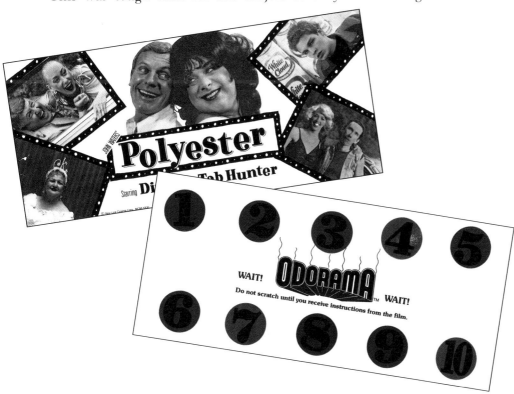

The big movie studios of the late fifties and early sixties were faced with dramatically declining audiences and resorted to extending the cinematic experience to senses previously (and since) left untouched, such as touch and smell - with gimmicks like Hallucinogenic Hypnovision and Smell-O-Vision. John Waters parodied these desperate methods in *Polyester* (1982), where a scratch'n'sniff card was distributed to audiences to whiff at pertinent points in the movie. Some of the smells were not those that you would expect to pay good money to experience.

A teenage Titan of terror on a lustful binge - audience identification with a film's hero has always been a major pull. Taking their lead from purveyors of pulp fiction, exploitation filmmakers soon learned that an arresting title, an extravagant strap line and a lurid poster were all you needed to sell entertainment.

filmmakers who were supple and flexible enough to stoop lower than previously thought possible.

The standard Hollywood genres of western, musical, thriller, comedy and war movie were aimed at too wide an audience for the exploitation film-makers to subvert. These genres had too many fixed rules and took too long to adapt to deal with the fast-changing contemporary themes that the teen audiences liked. An entire alternative set of genres was created - concerned mostly with sex, race, horror, motorcycles, drugs and beach parties. They concerned teenagers (obviously), rock'n'roll, juvenile delinquents, monsters, aliens, spies, detectives, bikers, communists, drugs, natural catastrophes, atomic bombs, the prehistoric past and the projected future. Their stars were has-beens of all types: ex-models, ex-sports stars, fading rock stars and would-be Marilyns.

One of the most successful of the exploitation filmmakers was Samuel Z. Arkoff, a lawyer from Iowa who together with James H. Nicholson, a cinema manager from the West coast, founded American Independent Pictures (AIP). The marque signified top-quality exploitation for over 20 years or more. They had a simple policy of dreaming up sensational titles for their films, such as *I Was A Teenage Werewolf, Invasion of the Saucermen* and *Highschool Hellcats*, then carried out some cursory market research with the cinema owners to see if they thought there would be a market for them. Arkoff and

Nicholson would then build their film around any title that scored a hit.

The extent of the depravity that the moralists claimed their films fostered can be seen from their plots. *Teenagers from Outer Space* (1959) describes how a young alien falls for a teenage earth girl and ruins the plans of his invading cohorts by blowing them up. The invaders, who arrived in a flying saucer, no less, carry ray guns and breed giant lobster monsters for food! The film's budget runs only to showing the shadow of one of these tasty crustaceans. *Horror of Party Beach* (1964) features kids on a beach dancing to 'The Zombie Stomp' and a girl who drinks hard liquor and strips for bikers. Meanwhile, radioactive waste turns human skulls on the bottom of the ocean into horrible monsters! They kill the wayward girl on the beach, then all the girls at the slumber party. If you still don't know what's happening, newspaper headlines ('MONSTERS STRIKE AGAIN!' and 'MASS MURDER AT SLUMBER PARTY') are shown to keep you informed. *Mondo Teeno* (1965) more than any other film explains the state of America today. Burt Topper narrates a pseudo-documentary as the young go mad (as they do) on sex, drugs, rock music and wild fashions.

With the turmoil of the Cold War, the Asian wars, and the general loosening of morals, the world to many kids in the fifties and sixties was a threatening and confusing place, and in some of the films the cosy certainties of life are undermined by the inexplicable or the alien. But other films set about reinforcing that cosiness, with a vengeance. For example, in *How to Stuff a Wild Bikini* (1965) Frankie Avalon features as a naval reserve on duty in Tahiti. He doesn't trust his girlfriend, played by another erstwhile pop star, Annette Funicello, to stay faithful, so he hires a witch-doctor (played by the 70-year-old, and presumably desperate, Buster Keaton) to help. Keaton conjures up a floating bikini and 'stuffs' it with a girl who is then sent to distract one of Miss Funicello's suitors. In a similar vein, but measurably more wholesome, the British side of the Atlantic created pop music film vehicles for the teenybop stars of the day, such as Cliff Richard in *Expresso Bongo*, *The Young Ones* and *Summer Holiday*.

In the latter half of the swinging decade, when all young people without exception were, of course, 'freaking out', a different sort of movie was made to cater to their depraved taste, or alternatively to warn of the horrors of their behaviour. In antithesis to the naïvety of the beach-boy fun of just a few years previous, psychedelic drug movies such as *Mary Jane* (exposing the shocking facts behind the marijuana

Teenagers save the universe.

47

The beach was a popular location for many exploitation movies of the early sixties, with films enjoying such alluring titles as *How to Stuff a Wild Bikini, The Horror of Party Beach* (above and top right) and *Beach Blanket Bingo*. The movie makers knew their audience for, whether you were practising your surfing technique or fighting Rockers, the beach was the place to be if you were a teenager. The dance here is the Zombie Stomp.

controversy), *The Love-Ins* and *The Hallucination Generation* depict young people as no more than strange hairstyles and clothes that dig hippies, yippies and loud rock music. *The Love-Ins* (1967) stars Richard Todd as a Timothy Leary-type ex-professor. He becomes a self-centred idol, wearing robes and advocating LSD. After he gets one of his followers pregnant, her ex-boyfriend assassinates the new messiah at a rally in a stadium. The film's satanic energy is such that it was banned in the UK.

SCHLOCK AND SPLATTER

There's a whole host of horror films which contain the most unbelievable plots and fine examples of ham acting. For example, any movie from the Hammer studios, and much of Roger Corman's work, will provide a study of bad taste in the movies, but for pure unadulterated kitsch in this genre, you need to make a visit to the outer limits of filmmaking, in the low budget and tacky sub-genre that has recently been categorised as 'schlock-horror'.

48

Herschell Gordon-Lewis is the self-styled 'Guru of Gore' and claims to be the first person to show people dying with their eyes open! In *Blood Feast* (1963), a Playboy brunette has her brains scooped out from her skull and a blonde has her tongue pulled out. This particular piece of gore was made all the more spectacular with the aid of a new film-processing technique that Lewis had developed called 'Blood Color'. This fine fellow went on to make a number of other gore classics, *2000 Maniacs* (dismemberment, a human barbecue, a ride in a barrel lined with nails), *The Gruesome Twosome* (live scalpings to make wigs) and *She-Devils On Wheels* (decapitation, orgy, and pre-dating Fay Weldon by 20 years!).

Lewis' explicit and unique movies were the forefathers of the unpleasant 'Splatter' horror sub-sub-genre of the seventies when such infamous sicko-thrillers as *I Spit on Your Grave* and *Driller Killer* helped along the decision to impose the standard Film Board Classifications on videotapes. Despite their crude gore, Lewis' films have a comic element in high-camp performances, absurd storylines and the most bizarre and imaginative deaths which elevate them above much of the mire that constitutes this area of filmmaking.

CONSCIOUS AND UNCONSCIOUS MASTERS

Other classic trash movie makers of the seventies worth checking out are Ray Dennis Steckler, who made weird and dreadful films with fabulous titles like *The Incredibly Strange Creatures Who Stopped*

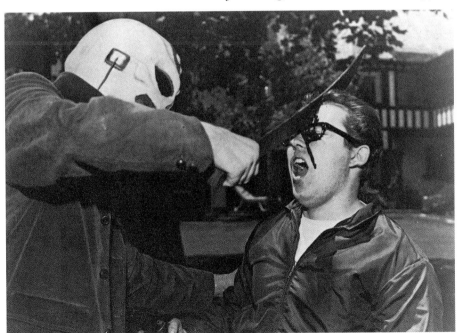

entre partings are in this year. On the outer limits of film-making there exists a tacky sub-genre known as Schlock Horror. If you can prise your hands away from your eyes and cope with the crude gore, it can provide an absolute treasure trove, characterised by hammy acting, absurd storylines and grotesquely improbable butchery. Equally obligatory, of course, are the outrageous titles - such as *The Corpse Grinders*, *The Astro-Zombies* (left) and, best of all, *The Incredibly Strange Creatures Who Stopped Living and Became Mixed-Up Zombies.*

Living and Became Mixed-Up Zombies (filmed in Terrorama!), a Batman and Robin spoof called, inexplicably, *Rat Pfink A Boo Boo* and *The Lemon Grove Kids Meet The Monsters*. Ted V. Mikels was another low budget schlock-horror king, helming the sci-fi-themed *The Astro Zombies, The Doll Squad* and *The Corpse Grinders* on budgets that were below comprehension. Another filmmaker worth noting here is a lady called Doris Wishman who was a kitsch phenomenon in her own right. She began by making films about nudist camps (*Nature Camp Confidential* and *Blaze Starr Goes Nudist*) and peaked in more than just exploitation terms when in the early seventies she teamed up with sex star Chesty Morgan to make two sexploitation classics, *Deadly Weapons* and *Double Agent '73*. The latter was so named because 73 was the measurement in inches of Chesty's bust. The former also refers to those mammaries, which in this case are put to use by their owner to asphyxiate various men in revenge for the sexual abuse she suffered in childhood from her father.

Most of these filmmakers were working on a scale of production that was little above home-movie. Indeed many actually financed their own ventures and some of them did very well out of it. Some are still making the odd film to this day. Possibly the strangest of all these characters in this particular annal of cinematic kitsch is an eccentric individual called Ed Wood Jr. Wood plumbed the nadir of kitsch

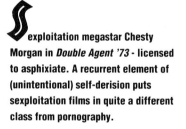

exploitation megastar Chesty Morgan in *Double Agent '73* - licensed to asphixiate. A recurrent element of (unintentional) self-derision puts sexploitation films in quite a different class from pornography.

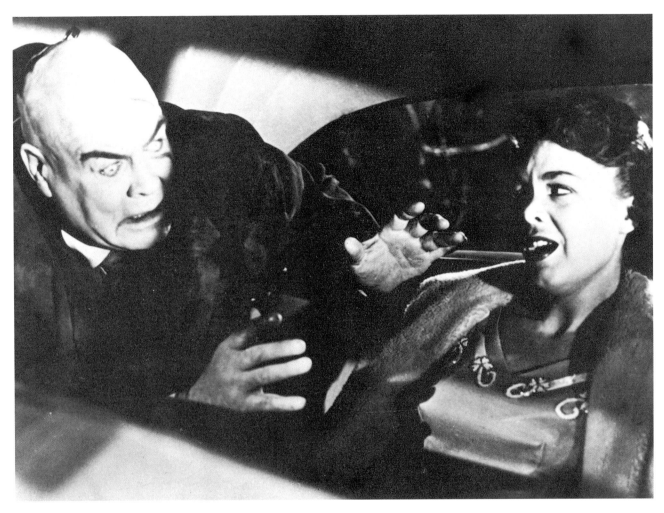

movie-making probably without ever knowing what the word meant. His films were made entirely in black and white, which adds to the quality of other-worldliness that they all possess. He worked across the genres: a western, *Crossroads Avenger*; a crime melodrama, *Jailbait*; sexploitation, *Glen or Glenda* (Wood himself was a transvestite); and even science fiction, *Bride of The Atom* and his best-known picture, *Plan Nine from Outer Space*. This film is a classic which mainly earned its status from its stunningly bizarre continuity errors: a black car would suddenly become a white car when the scene cut to a different angle, and day would switch to night during the same sequence.

None of this seemed to matter to Wood, who made decisions that bordered on the insane. For instance, when Bela Lugosi, his star of *Plan Nine*, died after just a few days' shooting, he replaced him with his chiropodist, who played the part for the remainder of the film with a cape drawn across his face. Unfortunately, the chiropodist was nearly a foot taller than Lugosi. With such inspiration behind it, it is not

A scene from *Plan Nine from Outer Space* - often voted the worst film of all time. It is rife with the crudest continuity errors and such ingenuous budget-saving devices as using hubcaps and paper cups for flying saucers. When his star died director Ed Wood Jr had no compunction about using the original footage and shooting the rest of the film with an actor who was a foot taller. At one point two men dressed as pilots sit in front of a bare wall and simply pretend they are in the cockpit of a plane!

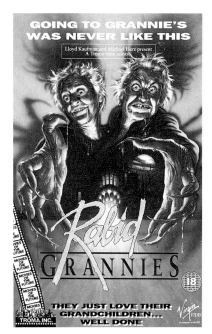

Troma Films movies are produced for the drive-in equivalent of the nineties, the VCR. They follow in the grand tradition of exploitation movies, especially in the titles such as *Surf Nazis Must Die* and *Fat Guy Goes Nutzoid*, and they have even created their very own superhero, the Toxic Avenger.

surprising that *Plan Nine* has been heralded as the worst film ever made – but boring it certainly isn't. If kitsch is poor-quality foisted upon the public in the hope that they won't notice, Wood is its beggar king.

The quality end of the exploitation tradition is being kept alive and well today by Troma Films, a production company located in the New York neighbourhood of Hell's Kitchen. The brainchild of two Yale graduates and trash movie nuts, Lloyd Kaufman and Michael Herz, Troma have successfully exploited the demand for low-budget tailor-made tongue-in-cheek films for videotape rental and cinemas in Far Eastern markets, where they will watch anything as long as it has a high enough sex and violence quotient.

Troma deserve an Oscar for their titles alone. Who can resist the following at the local video rental store: *Surf Nazis Must Die, Fat Guy Goes Nutzoid, Demented Death Farm Massacre, I Was A Teenage TV Terrorist, The Class of Nuke 'Em High* and their most successful creation, *The Toxic Avenger*? 'Toxie', as he is affectionately known, is a deformed cult hero - a one time sand-faced wimp who, after exposure to toxic waste, becomes Troma's own Indiana Jones combining gross-out with environmental awareness. The Green Giant of exploitation now has three movies behind him and a future beyond his creators' wildest dreams. In the best exploitation tradition, *Toxic Avenger 1* cost under $1m and has so far grossed just over $15m, making Troma a major force in American independent cinema.

Troma encourage new talent - Kevin Costner's first film was a Troma release – and they also uphold moral standards. 'Our movies are positive and wholesome,' claims Lloyd Kaufman. 'We never had a hero that takes drugs or fools around if he's married. Many films for young people are cynical and the audience is expected to sympathise with the film's bad protagonist. We're not like that at Troma.' I did say that a sense of comedy was an element in the Troma oeuvre, didn't I?

SEXPLOITATION

The cinema discovered that sex equalled cash at about the same time as it realised that people would pay good money to watch stories told by moving pictures. On the whole, sex and sex appeal provided the prime motif of Hollywood films in the twenties, but while this was good for the box office it had unwanted side effects, for Hollywood gave itself a reputation as being a sink of iniquity.

Scandals involving sex and drugs like the Fatty Arbuckle affair and the murder of William Drummond Taylor, set against the steamy silent output of Cecil B. De Mille or the endless victim movies that starred Lillian Gish, threw the industry into a mild panic. Fearing that its affairs might come under the scrutiny of a federal investigation, Hollywood set up its own censorship office under a man called William Hays. Hays, who was made the president of a newly formed Motion Picture Producers and Distributors Association of America, was a severe man who took his job of cleaning up Hollywood very seriously indeed. He believed firmly that movies should be mass entertainment, and disapproved of anything unsuitable for a family audience.

The Hays Code introduced in 1927 reads today as an essential part of the literature of kitsch. A list of do's and don'ts co-drafted with the

Despite the pernicious endeavours of the Hollywood censorship office, headed by William Hays, to suppress the human libido, female sexuality fought back strongly, with actresses like Joan Crawford, Barbara Stanwyck, Greta Garbo, and, here, Jean Harlow. The code made the mistake of only prescribing certain actions; it contained some glaring omissions, such as forgetting to ban sitting enticingly in a chair.

53

representatives of the Catholic Church included such directives as no on-screen mouth-to-mouth kissing, single beds even for married couples, and all love scenes to be enacted with both partners having at least one foot on the floor. Under its strictures a scene showing labour pains was deleted from *Way Down East*.

Despite Hays' attempts to eliminate any reference to the naughty parts in thirties films, the human libido fought back, and in no uncertain terms. Female sexuality was on offer from a variety of sources - Crawford, Stanwyck, Shearer, Colbert and Garbo. A particular type of bold female became very popular - the blonde sexpot. One of the most spectacular of these early bimbettes was Jean Harlow. On screen she was flashy and tarty, the original platinum blonde. It was said that she even dyed her pubic hair the same colour because allegedly she never wore underwear and didn't want a kind of five o'clock shadow peeping through. Her great forte as an actress was to make sex funny and comedy sexy, in which she was the direct forerunner of Marilyn Monroe.

But the most significant sex queen of pre-1950s Hollywood was undoubtedly Mae West. Already 41 when she hit the big time, she was at an age that would today put her in the same bracket as all the other old boilers who are so-called sex symbols on TV - Joan Collins, Kate O'Mara and Linda Evans — but back in 1933 a woman over the age of 30 was considered to be well and truly dried up. Mae West proved common opinion wrong when her two biggest movies, *She Done Him Wrong* and *I'm No Angel*, literally saved her studio, Paramount, from liquidation. Their appeal was explicit - when studio head Adolph Zukor read the line 'hitting the highpoints of lusty entertainment' in the poster for the former he complained to his publicity man about the use of the word 'lusty'. The PR guy cleverly replied that 'lusty' was derived from the German word 'lustig' meaning 'jolly' or 'merry'. Zukor listened patiently, sighed and said, 'One look at that dame's tits and I know what the word "lusty" means.'

Mae West was a pioneer. Her personality was a celebration of sexuality and she made sex acceptable for its own sake with no nonsense or bullshit. Her behaviour was camply gauche, and even today women are not expected to be so upfront about sex. Although her films themselves are not kitsch - at least the early films before the Hays Code clamped down on her explicitness - she was to be an enormous influence on the queens of sleaze that followed her.

The prominent chest has been the cornerstone of many a successful Hollywood career - Jane Russell, Marilyn Monroe, Kim Novak, Ann

Mae West sold her sexuality with the subtlety of a fairground barker. Although her films are far too clever and self-aware to be kitsch, she created the model for cheaper imitations that lacked her irony. *I'm No Angel* (above) rescued Paramount from near-bankruptcy.

Margret, Sophia Loren, Bette Midler and Dolly Parton, to name just a handful. In the fifties an hourglass figure became essential for any would-be screen goddess. For a short while it seemed, the bigger the better.

Screenwriter George Axelrod (who among other things scripted *The Seven Year Itch* and *The Manchurian Candidate*) had a young actress under personal contract and made a screen test of her. The climax came with the girl rubbing one of her not inconsiderable breasts gently against the camera! The starlet in question was the legendary Jayne Mansfield - ten out of ten on the kitsch scale and her career hadn't even begun yet.

This sex bomb is certainly one of the most potent icons ever produced by Hollywood. Her bosom appeared not only to defy

Jayne Mansfield lived her life in the style of a goddess of kitsch. As a legendary blonde sex bomb of the silver screen, her sex appeal lay not in the coyness of Harlow, but in the highly charged female sexuality of Monroe. Her ultimate bimbo act caused her to become one of the world's most famous personalities of the late fifties.

55

Newton's laws of gravity but also contravened Einstein's theory of relativity. Her hair was the platinum blonde of Jean Harlow (her heroine, incidentally) and her sex appeal lay not in coyness but in the highly-charged female sexuality of Marilyn Monroe. Jayne was simply peroxide personified, her body literally seemed to be bursting out of whatever she wore. She never understood the art of the understatement, but was the queen of over-the-top.

Jayne Mansfield's physique, her ultimate bimbo act and her liaison with George Axelrod caused her to become one of the most famous personalities in the world in the late fifties, but, strangely, her movies were few and little seen. In fact probably only one in a hundred fans would have ever seen her act and that would certainly have been her most successful movie, *The Girl Can't Help It* of 1957.

The plot of this dramatic masterpiece has Tom Ewell as a talent agent who becomes a drunk after his main client, a crooning songstress, played by Julie London, leaves him. Then he meets a gangster who assigns him to turn his girlfriend, played by Jayne, into a star. Unfortunately, Jayne has a voice like an air-raid siren, but her figure more than makes up for it. Her first record is a hit, but there's still trouble, as she's fallen in love with Ewell. There is, of course, a happy ending: Ewell becomes a rock'n'roll star and Jayne quits performing to marry him. Every scene of this great movie has the stamp of Frank Tashlin, the director, who bombards his audience with sight gags - as Jayne walks down the street in the opening scene, the caps pop off milk bottles and windows and eyeglasses shatter.

Jayne Mansfield lived her life in the style of a goddess of kitsch. She learned about the photo opportunity as career move early on, upstaging Jane Russell and Sophia Loren respectively - the latter was caught in a memorable image with her eyes popping out at the sight of Jayne's cleavage. When she visited the UK in 1955, a photographer managed to catch her going upstairs from below. Like Harlow, she never wore underwear and her fanny was subsequently emblazoned on all the front pages of Europe. She remained philosophical, 'There's an old adage I learned in Hollywood: as long as they spell your name right...'

At the height of her fame she created the notorious Pink Palace on Sunset Boulevard, out of the former home of silent-film star Rudy Vallee. Painted in her own not-too delicate shade of Mansfield Pink, the interiors featured heart-shaped beds, bathtubs and a swimming pool with 'I Love You Jayney' tiled into the floor by second husband Mickey Hargitay; there was also a Press Room hung with 500 framed

John Waters once described her as the world's first female female-impersonator. Peroxide personified and bursting out of whatever dress she was put in, Jayne Mansfield was famous for being every inch herself. The films she made were forgotten almost as soon as they were released. They were not helped by her singing voice, especially as it was often called upon, as in this nightclub scene from *Too Hot to Handle* (right). But she was also known as the smartest dumb blonde in the world - she had degrees from the universities of both Texas and California, and her IQ outpaced even her bosom at a measurement of 163.

magazine covers featuring the busty blonde. In a cute twist of kitsch history, the Pink Palace is now home to one of Jayne's former suitors, Englebert Humperdinck (real name Gerry Dorsey), crooning king of the sweaty, middle-aged knicker-throwing Las Vegas circuit.

Mansfield died tragically, gruesomely decapitated in an automobile accident in which she was driving. In the year before her death, the girl who once sold her bathwater for $10 a bottle to adoring fans was the judge for a transvestite Jayne Mansfield lookalike contest - the ultimate kitsch accolade.

At approximately the same time that Jayne was making her mark, another figure was taking the celluloid ideal of the female figure from the sublime to the ridiculous. The son of a policeman and a nurse who had worked her way through six husbands, Russ Meyer filled his movies with some of the largest-breasted women to have walked the earth. The frequency with which big bouncing boobs appear on-screen

The buxom wenches who grace these two pages are stars from the films of the king of sexploitation, Russ Meyer. The busts of his stars like Kitten Natividad (below) left bra makers in despair.

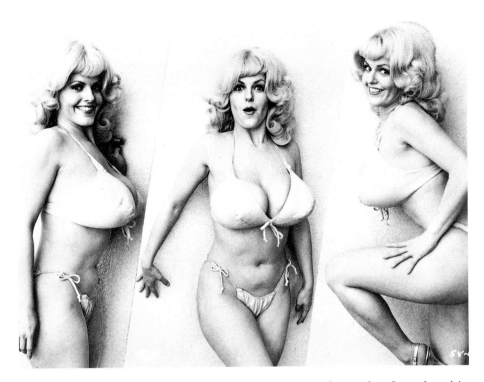

in his movies, however, often distracts viewers from the fact that his films present serious socio-critical content and complex moral dilemmas. Well they would, wouldn't they?

Meyer was responsible for something of a major breakthrough for sex in the cinema when his film *The Immoral Mr Teas* became the first soft core porno flick to return a huge profit - an investment of some $24,000 brought back over a million dollars. This was a trigger for the major studios to show serious interest in Mr Meyer. After he returned a $6 million profit on the $76,000 budget of another crude tit-pic, *Vixen*, he was signed by 20th Century Fox to produce two of his feebler efforts on sex and violence themes, *Beyond the Valley of the Dolls* (1970) and *Seven Minutes* (1971).

Meyer is credited by sympathetic critics as being a major force for advancing sexual freedom, but what he really did was to pave the way almost single-handedly for the entire nudie-cutie genre and later hardcore films that continue to this day. But it's worth catching at least one of Meyer's films, such as *Faster Pussycat Kill! Kill!*, *Mud Honey* or *Lorna* if only for the spectacle of these balloon-like appendages springing about vigorously in pursuit of some didactic storyline.

THE PRINCE OF PUKE

'Exploitation films are the only ones that come close to the dreaded word "art". I still wonder why film students babble on about Orson

Welles or Howard Hawks when they ignore the greatest masters in film history: Russ Meyer and Herschell Gordon Lewis. Even the worst films by these two directors are infinitely more interesting than *Citizen Kane*.' These are the words of John Waters, the King of Movie Kitsch, or as he prefers it, the Prince of Puke. 'To me, bad taste is what entertainment is all about. If someone vomits during one of my films it's like getting a standing ovation!'

Waters is probably the most celebrated bad taste filmmaker in the world. He set out deliberately to offend the sensibilities of his audience and consciously to create kitsch, in contrast to his idols whose kitsch was created by happy accident. He stands in an important position on the road which starts with kitsch as an intended product, through the half-knowing creation of kitsch, to its deliberate and overt self-declaration. That the trash aesthetic is now accepted by the mainstream is shown by the fact that the man who set out to subvert American society through his cinema was invited to make a film, *Cry Baby*, by Universal Pictures. By having the backing of major Hollywood studio, the ultimate irony is now a tantalising possibility - he could one day be in line for an Oscar!

Waters' most celebrated movie, *Pink Flamingos*, made in 1972, is a true classic - the film in which bad taste in the cinema really broke the ice with the public, although it took some years for it to get a release. Perhaps this isn't surprising with a storyline that concerns two groups of outcasts vying for the title of 'The Filthiest People Alive'. On one side we have Waters' own sexbomb, a gigantic transvestite, Divine, and her troubled family that includes Edith Massey as a 250lb senior citizen who sits in a child's playpen dressed in a girdle and bra and worships eggs. The challengers to the title are Connie and Raymond Marble (Mink Stole and David Lothary), a jealous publicity-hungry couple with pre-punk green and red hair who sell heroin to inner-city school children and kidnap hitch-hiking girls, impregnating them with their manservant's semen and selling the babies to lesbian couples.

The Divine family is trying to live quietly, knowing that they are indeed 'the filthiest people alive', but the Marbles attempt to seize this title by sending them a turd in the post and burning the mobile home they all live in to the ground. Provoked into war, the Divine entourage kidnaps the Marbles, puts them on public trial for 'assholism' and murders them at a press conference called for the sleaziest newspapers in the country. In the final scene of the uncensored version of the film, Divine eats a hot and fresh doggy turd (it's not faked on screen) to reclaim her rightful title before she moves the family to Idaho to

Self-styled Prince of Puke John Waters - always on the look-out for top-grade trash.

return to a peaceful filthy existence.

This is the trash aesthetic in its most extreme guise. When Waters says things like, 'One must remember that there is such a thing as good Bad taste and bad Bad taste', he's being serious. 'It's easy to disgust. I could easily make a 90 minute film about people getting their legs hacked off, but this would only be bad Bad taste and not very stylish or original. Good Bad taste can be nauseating but must, at the same time, be appealing to the especially twisted sense of humour.' Beneath all the outrage, everything Waters does is driven by a sense of comedy. You just require that twist in your sense of humour and strong stomach lining to appreciate it.

John Waters works at the hard core of kitsch, his frame of reference determined by his home town Baltimore, Maryland, which he characterised as 'the hairdo capital of the world'. From an early age he fell in love with low-rent exploitation films and was particularly fascinated by their amateurish look, their predilection with social dilemmas, and the gore.

From this obsession with the tacky side of life, Waters concocted his first movie in 1964, the wonderfully titled *Hag in a Black Leather Jacket.* He had two aims: to establish himself as a kind of sleazoid Andy Warhol and to jolt the middle classes from whence he came. He made four more films before he was to transverse the peaks of kitsch with *Pink Flamingos*; the last of these, *Multiple Maniacs* (1970), was inspired by one of Waters' little personal obsessions in life, the notorious Manson Family slaying of Sharon Tate and her houseguests in California in 1968.

In 1982 he wrote and directed possibly his finest and funniest movie, successfully taking the trash aesthetic to the masses with *Polyester*. Divine stars as Francine Fishpaw, a housewife whose life is a shambles because of her cheating porno-theatre-owner husband, her glue-sniffing, angel-dusting son, and her wild pregnant daughter. Her only friend is her retarded ex-maid, played by Edith Massey. She drinks herself into a constant stupor and her dog commits suicide. But her life perks up when a handsome playboy, played by B-movie matinee idol Tab Hunter, shows up. Filled with references to exploitation, pornography and art movies, this should have been Waters' greatest hit, but the humour in this bid for mass acceptance proved a little too close to the bone. Waters used shock tactics throughout his career, until he no longer needed to make such loud noises and was chased by the independent New York-based production company, New Line Cinema, who financed the very successful

Waters' *Female Trouble* charts the career of the less-than-lithe Dawn Davenport from juvenile delinquent through hooker to mass murderer and the electric chair. This, for her, is the final accolade, the recognition that she has reached the top of her profession.

61

Hairspray in 1987.

In his later movies Waters displayed his acute and unique sense of kitsch in ever-increasing sophistication. No-one understands the comic value of creative casting as well as he; half-dead rock stars (Stiv Bators in *Polyester*), forgotten B-movie stars (Tab Hunter in the same film), fading pop stars (Debbie Harry in *Hairspray*), ex-soft porn stars (Pia Zadora in the same picture), or underage ex-hardcore stars (Traci Lords in *Cry Baby*). But the mainstay of Waters' casts until his untimely death in 1988 was Waters' very own version of Jayne Mansfield, Divine.

THE MOST BEAUTIFUL WOMAN IN THE WORLD

In real life an ex-hairdresser christened Glenn Muldoon, Divine is one reason for Waters' immense popularity; the other is their joint sense of mischievousness. Divine also grew up in the hairdo capital of the world, living just a block away from Waters. Although they weren't really friends, they picked up on each others' vibes in their formative years.

As a child, Divine worshipped Elizabeth Taylor and vowed one day to be a star. Harassed viciously by schoolchums, he realised quite early on that this goal was not going to be easy to achieve. Deep down he knew he was the most beautiful woman in the world, but how could he convince the rest of us?

Divine somehow sensed that his career was not going anywhere until the press outside of Baltimore began to notice his early films. As soon as he tasted the publicity, he found himself. He headed straight for California, went out every night and eventually got his picture in *Time* magazine in full drag. In the early seventies he spent a lot of time in San Francisco doing stage shows at the Palace Theatre with titles such as 'Divine and her Stimulating Studs', 'Divine Saves the World' and 'Vice Palace'. When he heard that *Pink Flamingos* was opening in Los Angeles, he relocated to Santa Monica and arrived at the premiere on the back of a garbage truck. He held court on the beach daily and the word quickly got around that you just had to see Divine in a string bikini. He would confuse the press by saying 'Gay? Are you kidding? I've got a wife and two kids back in Omaha.'

In an ultimate kitsch scenario, he schemed his way into the mansions of Bel-Air where he was happiest lounging around the private swimming pools. Sometimes he would crash the most fashionable parties, and as soon as the host recognised the infamous drag, another door to fame was opened. Big stars began to notice,

It's somewhat ironic that the movie star that Divine (née plain old Glen Muldoon) idolised as a child, Liz Taylor, has subsequently set out to emulate his legendarily bloated physique!

although some, like Ann Margret, could only do a double-take and blurt: 'What the...how hideous!'

Divine was no transvestite, simply a man cast as a woman, who regarded his flamboyant outfits as his work clothes. He was a high camp anti-hero, whose cock-eyed glamour act was a subversive interpretation of the whole sexbomb trip. Behind the front he believed himself to be a serious actor, who in the line of duty was prepared to eat dog turds, crawl through pig shit, mainline eyeliner and risk arrest by appearing in Waters' films.

THE TRIUMPH OF TRASH

When the whole notion of enjoying bad taste became popular in the late seventies, genre analyses, structuralism and auteur theories were abandoned by some cinéastes in favour of new cinematic erogenous zones. A growing section of the public was bored with the concept of good cinema and was now watching and enjoying films so bad it seems hard to believe they were ever made.

In 1979 and 1980, two American brothers, Harry and Michael Medved, published a pair of immensely successful books dedicated to trash movies - *The Fifty Worst Movies of All Time* and *The Golden Turkey Awards*. A vast body of films that had previously been disregarded because they didn't meet certain standards of direction, acting, sets, dialogue, continuity or whatever were pushed into the limelight, but mainstream Hollywood productions were not exempt from inclusion either as 'Golden Turkeys'. For example, the Medveds voted special 'Life Achievement' Awards to Raquel Welch as the Worst Actress of all time (possibly understandable) and Richard Burton as the Worst Actor.

A number of cinemas began to capitalise upon on this enthusiasm for turkeys by programming the 'so bad they're good' movies. At the Scala cinema in London's seedy Kings Cross and St Marks theatre on New York's equally dodgy Lower East Side fights frequently broke out

The Zucker-Abrahams-Zucker team's 1980 masterpiece *Airplane* was a satirical anthology of cliches from bad movies.

in the struggle for admission to all-night screenings. In 1984, a TV series was created based upon the Medveds' books and the cult of the trash film was transmitted to a mass audience. This celebration of pulp has been going on ever since, with numerous books and TV series, the best and most intelligent being Jonathon Ross' 'Incredibly Strange Film Show' series and Michael Wheldon's indispensible magnum opus of a guide to trashy movies, *The Psychotronic Encyclopaedia of Film*. Even the previously very stuffy British National Film Theatre has screened a season of 'Schlock' movies in response to what it calls its 'new and wider programming philosophy'. Blimey.

The trash aesthetic has not just won a loyal audience for itself but has now worked its way into the heart of Hollywood. The influence of the Other History of Cinema can be seen in the work of a number of younger film-makers who are leading the way in comedy. The Zucker-Abrahams-Zucker team responsible for such comic classics as *Airplane 1* and *2* and *The Naked Gun*, draw their stilted dialogue and contrived characters and storylines from the trash disaster movies that were popular in the late seventies. Julian Temple's *Earth Girls are Easy* (1988) is in itself a fundamentally kitsch concept. The musical, science fiction and sloppy romance genres are fused in it, and are all delivered in the most self-conscious B-movie style. Finally, if John Waters' *Cry Baby* is far less extreme than his non-Hollywood movies, at least the bad taste aesthetic is visible in every frame.

Does this embracing of kitsch indicate the ultimate victory or final defeat for Hollywood? Will it quickly exhaust it and then toss it aside, or is it the desperate attempt by a drowning industry to clutch at another straw? Look at it one way, by absorbing the kitsch movies that it did so much to create, Hollywood has absorbed what was specifically set up to be distinct from it, like some mega-corporation buying up a smaller but troublesome rival. Look at it another way, and it is an implicit and potentially fatal admission that the values and standards propounded in Hollywood's films are, always were and ever shall be irredeemably bogus.

Or maybe we should look at this a third way. Perhaps it is another slippery twist from that serpentine beast, kitsch - a new kitsch phenomenon of bad taste that exploits bad taste and is produced by those who pretend that they haven't got the good taste to pull it off, when in fact it's a cynical exercise in the name of making money, hence fundamentally bad taste...

SCHLOCK AROUND THE CLOCK

Selling a couple of million records doesn't satisfy megastars these days as merchandising spin-offs can account for more of an artist's earnings than recording and songwriting royalties. This is the reason why they seem quite content to see their own likeness flogged to death on all kinds of dodgy objects from mugs and scarves to pillow cases, jigsaw puzzles and even dolls.

The music business over-exploits its product and markets probably more than any other branch of the entertainment industry. In no other industry (except possibly fashion) is so much energy put into spotting, manufacturing, marketing and selling new trends and short-term fashions, but the results of all this human effort are no more than a binful of chewed-up, spat-out and half-digested images and music. Maybe the music business ran out of ideas years ago. Certainly, there must be some reason why the grizzlier elements of pop history refuse to lie down, like a corpse in a horror movie. The out-of-date clothes and hairstyles of half-forgotten teenybop groups such as Dave Dee, Dozy, Beaky, Mick and Tich, The Rubettes, Flintlock, Buck's Fizz and Kenny are sadly only that - no more than half-forgotten. They still clutter record store remainder bins where they exercise that flypaper charm of classic kitsch, repelling and attracting at the same time.

The ghastly appeal of this old kitsch pop lies in the fact that the very strength of the nostalgia that music arouses within us means you can now like records that at the time of their original release you dismissed as trash. I bet that many of the 'Golden Oldies' radio stations are listened to by middle-aged people who enjoy records half of which they dismissed at the time as rubbish, but which they now find bring back warm memories of their youth.

Pop music is fundamentally kitsch because it is totally phony and disposable. Just take a look at the self-consciousness and narcissism evident in the poses of any self-invented pop music personality. From the bogus futurism of Gary Numan to the cock-rock braggadocio of the likes of Ozzy Osbourne and Kiss, all the way to the aggressively sexed-up iconography that Madonna now espouses, the image of the pop star has in many cases become more important than the actual music.

It has long been recognised that the machinery of hype in pop music is infinitely more important than any real creativity. During pop's brief history, record pluggers have become central to the success of almost any song, and not surprisingly a cynical insincerity pervades the entire business. It is a sentiment that courses its way from the bullish methodology of the cartel of record company boardrooms through to their A&R and marketing departments, as they ruthlessly exploit both their precious artistes and the punters whose disposable incomes keep the industry fat. Much music is not created by the musicians at all but by the record companies and their producers, who know, or think they know, what will appeal to mass taste.

Every so often, the music industry's belief in itself is humiliatingly exposed, as in the debacle surrounding Milli Vanilli in 1990. The group was awarded and later ignominiously stripped of the music business version of an Oscar, an Emmy, when it was revealed that they didn't even sing on their records, let alone have a hand in the composition of the music. Marketed as musicians, they were merely good-looking dancers. But what is most interesting is not the sad subterfuge, but the fact that in the eyes of their comrades in the business, the record

Pop moguls always think it's the image that counts . The Village People were originally fairly distinctive and more-than-averagely inspired, but in a misguided attempt to move with the times they adopted the New Romantic look in the early eighties.

Doris Day (top) was early proof of the durability of mindlessly undemanding pop against the dangerous challenge of more spirited forms of music, with her big 1956 hit, 'Whatever Will Be, Will Be', at a time when rock'n'roll was supposed to be rampant. The Carpenters (above) maintained the tradition through the early seventies.

company seemed to have got it so right that the group was given the award in the first place.

ONWARD FROM THE PHONEYGRAPH

Although the ripping off of other people's music has been going on since the first time someone wrote down a hummable tune, it was the invention of the record player or phonograph as it was then called, by Thomas Edison in 1877 that really laid the foundations for corruption and exploitation. For the next 50 years all types of music were scratched into millions of wax cylinders and flat discs - by 1928 it was estimated that there were more than 2.5 million record players in Britain, with an even larger number in the USA.

The business had grown rapidly, and was to grow even more after the circuits of sound reproduction were dramatically expanded by the introduction of radio. Initially, the basis of the music industry in the early part of this century was professional song writing. Before royalties were paid to songwriters from the sales of records and airplays, songwriters and music publishers made their money through sheet music sales. In order to reach the public, professional 'pluggers' were dispatched to persuade famous stars to adopt the songs and department store salespeople to push them. Those who accepted were recompensed, naturally with drinks, dinners and gifts. In 1892, composer Charles K. Harris paid J. Aldrich Libby to put 'After the Ball' (generally held to be the first 'pop' song) in his musical *A Trip to Chinatown*. That great hit of 1923, 'Yes, We Have No Bananas' involved many hands in Tin Pan Alley - it was 'plugged' and promoted relentlessly until it became a hit. Music publishers would also get several artists to record a song, because the more versions were being played, the more often the song was being dangled in front of the sheet music-buying public.

The blatant pursuit of manipulation of a record's success through covert bribery became more sophisticated as musical reproduction became more advanced technologically. Disc jockeys, so-called because they 'rode' certain records up the charts, were hassled or bribed to play particular numbers endlessly until the public bought the records in the hope of exorcising the wretched tunes from their minds.

Not even Hollywood has as tarnished an image as the music business. Squeaky clean, it's not. Without even considering the exploits of recent rock stars, think of the many payola scandals over the years, culminating in the conviction in 1960 of America's most poular and influential DJ, Alan Freed, for having received in excess of $30,000.

But like Hollywood, the product itself has generally pretended to a

The Bay City Rollers were all pretence: their name was meant to suggest California, but this Edinburgh-based group even regarded Glasgow as foreign territory. Critics did not complain so much that they did not play on their own records but that they could not even lip synch accurately on TV. Maybe it was a shrewd understanding of the public's long-established weakness for strips of tartan that ensured their appeal, or else people had just given up listening to the records they bought, for a string of rum-tee-tum ditties made them by the mid-seventies the biggest Pop phenomenon in the UK since the Beatles.

state of saintliness, and herein lies the kitsch at the heart of Tin Pan Alley. While vast sums could be made out of music for the outlay of a few unseen readies, the songs in question painted pictures of a pure and simple world, where it snows every Christmas, the moon is always full, and the greatest crime in the world is to cheat on your girlfriend. Nothing sells as well as innocence, with a good lashing of sentiment.

It would be cosy to believe that all this is a thing of the past. The record industry may well have acted to reduce the opportunities of payola in the wake of the Alan Freed trial (in which he was being

69

made the scapegoat for a nationwide practice), but the suspicions are strong that more than one record has been made a hit by fortuitously heavy buying at the shops that provide the statistics for the charts. Even if we discount such theories as the products of jealous and petty-minded individuals, there is no business to match music for flying lawsuits. They come winging in alike from aggrieved singers suing ex-managers for vanished earnings, and from the Big Boys putting the frighteners on each other or on outsiders who foolishly cross their paths. Yet, even in the post-Punk era, the words and tunes of so many of the actual records are still as smooth and unspoilt as unwrapped bubblegum.

TEENYBOPPING KITSCH

Confusion, paranoia, insecurity and obsession with image - these are all traits of the music business. They are also the basic characteristics of its main customer for the last 40 years, the adolescent.

Some time in the early fifties, while carrying out its first market research into the tastes of the new teenage market, music industry bigwigs noticed that these teenagers liked to chew gum a lot. They responded by flooding the market with a music that was so sickly sweet and sticky that if it got in your hair it was a devil to get out.

Despite the arrival of rock'n'roll around about 1955, many of the big hits of the late fifties had little to do with swivelling hips and jiving but were unalloyed kitsch. For example 'The Purple People Eater' by Sheb Wooley (who played Pete Nolan in the TV series *Rawhide*) was a number one in the USA for five weeks in 1958, followed a few weeks later by the Italianate 'Volare'. Rock'n'roll itself gave teenagers a completely different sort of music, but it was not long before the music industry had tamed it into a softer, safer, non-rebellious form.

In its early days, teenybop music aimed itself at its target audience in the same opportunistic way as the quick-buck exploitation movie-makers had done - channelling its energies into the rapidly changing popular themes of the time: juvenile delinquency, beaches, fun and, eerily, death. Death, in particular provided a selection of songs that are appreciated as wonderful black comedy today. There was a mini-boom in the early sixties of apparently sincere musical odes to the very dearly departed. They range from simple dedications to the dead, such as 'Ebony Eyes' by the Everly Brothers through messages to those beyond the grave ('Tell Laura I Love Her' sung by Ray Peterson in 1960 and 'Terry' recorded by Twinkle in 1964), to vivid descriptions of

The nation wept buckets in 1964 when Twinkle sang of how her boyfriend Terry copped it on his motorbike.

70

the untimely demise of certain loved ones ('The Leader of the Pack' by the Shangri-La's and 'Dead Man's Curve' by Jan and Dean, both from 1964). Bloodrock's 'D.O.A. (Dead On Arrival)' of 1969 is in a class of its own and must genuinely be heard to be believed, it being the first person narration of an accident victim as he ebbs fast in the back of an ambulance whisking him vainly to hospital. Death often brings out kitsch in its most extreme form - a critical walk around the monuments in a graveyard, or a reading of the death of Little Nell in *The Old Curiosity Shop* will bear witness to this - and these songs truly revel in their own bad taste.

To the teenybopper kitsch does not exist, because the appreciation of kitsch is a sophisticated response that does not come instinctively. But, when the taste buds mature, the taste of our younger, less sophisticated selves is often a source of embarrassment to us. These naive former incarnations are often disowned as different beings - the possessions of youth either forgotten, left behind at the parental home or burnt in a ritual exorcising of youth. But the skeletons are unfortunately not bio-degradable and the ghosts of our adolescence will always be on hand to haunt us.

When looking back at this era of our lives we can all see the bad taste that may have existed within ourselves. For example, a balding thirtysomething may squirm at pictures of himself in the frills, bows and peek-a-boo fringes of the New Romantic fashion of the early eighties. But discriminating adults will react quite differently at parties. They will dance (and sing along in a very drunken and noisy manner) to the kitsch classics of their childhood. Depending on their age, fully grown feet have been known to twitch at 'Itsy Bitsy Teeny Weeny Yellow Polka-Dot Bikini' by Brian Hyland, 'Puppy Love' by Donny Osmond, 'Love Me, Love My Dog' by Peter Shelley, and anything by the Bay City Rollers, David Essex, T-Rex or the Wombles. In years to come you can expect that the same experience will be on hand for current fans of Bros, the New Kids on the Block and Jason Donovan.

BEWARE OF IMITATIONS

Fortunately we have been saved from an endless diet of junk music by the all-time greats haven't we? The early Elvis Presley, Bob Dylan, the Beatles, the Rolling Stones, the Who and the Grateful Dead gave us music that was safe to listen to, didn't they? But even the careers of these hallowed artists have not been without their own lapses into awfulness. The Beatles may be regarded by many as the best thing to happen to music since Mozart, but have you completely obliterated

Paul McCartney's twee and sickly 'Mary Had A Little Lamb' from your memory? As for the King, how about his mastery of the master race's mother tongue on 'Wooden Heart'? I won't go into the output of the others, as their fans have been known to be violent.

The music business, of course, wanted the success of the real rock phenomena to go on ad infinitum and with characteristic lack of imagination decided to try to repeat the formulas. Ignoring the implications of the fact that these stars had created their own style, the music industry turned mad scientist and tried to construct its own groups and singers in their image. Chemical corporations did it with new brands of soap powders, so why not the makers of soap music? But what they produced was all bubble and froth, without the power to clean deep down.

Once the hunt had been abandoned for another Elvis, the biggest prize became the next Beatles. Their phenomenal success and less than phenomenal wacky humour inspired the television subsidary of Columbia Pictures, Screen Gems, to audition actors and musicians to play the parts of a crazy pop group in a television series modelled on the offbeat style of the Beatles' films, *A Hard Day's Night* and *Help*. Swinging in from the lighting gantries came the Monkees, 'created' by film makers Bert Schneider and Bob Rafelson. It's not the music that earned them a place in the pantheon of kitsch - penned by some of the world's best-selling songwriters such as Neil Sedaka and Neil Diamond, much of it is quite good, if lacking in spontaneity. Their inclusion here stems instead from the medium for which they were created, their TV programme. These little situation comedies are funny only because they are so contrived. The music always came second.

Their stock situation each week was facing some earth-shatteringly banal or fanciful problem concerned with being in a group. For example, in one episode, their instruments have been stolen by a magic genie who had, naturally, appeared from an old pot innocently picked by one of the four loveable mop-tops. Obvious really. Their TV show is still staple late night 'so bad, it's good' viewing the world over.

With few exceptions, most great musical acts comprise singers and musicians who possess a natural chemistry that forms the basis of their talent. Attempts at recreating these magical characteristics in some misguided record company executive's mind only produce cheap and unconvincing imitations of the originals. Billy Fury, Marty Wilde, Reg Presley (and The Troggs), P. J. Proby and good old Cliff Richard were all poor men's Elvis Presleys, and despite all scoring hits and building considerable followings, they never quite got it right: the sneers were

Beatlemania spawned countless ways of cashing in, from musical imitations to myriad forms of merchandising. For a time it wasn't thought at all odd to have Paul and Ringo on your backside. If you ever wonder what Elvis would have looked like today take a look at Cliff Richard (below) who started life as Britain's answer to the King.

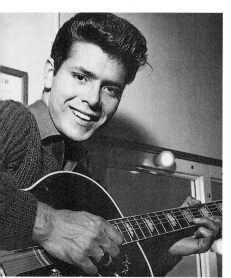

over-stated and their hips just didn't swivel in the same law-breaking way that the King's did. Reg Presley and P. J. Proby grossly overstated his smouldering sex appeal, and came across as sordid and rampant quasi-rapists. In Proby's case this meant ripping the seat of his too-tight pants at any (photo) opportunity. Cliff, on the other hand, soon dropped the gyrations and concentrated instead on the Elvis home-boy angle, but he was too clean and posed little sexual threat to the hordes of teenage girls eager for a scream. At least these guys got the hair

If it were not for the lurid stories of his private life, one could believe that the later Presley was self-fashioned as a savage satire on the whole kitsch world of pop stardom. The heavily paying audiences, though, loved him as he was, under the misguided impression that they were seeing the real Elvis.

almost right; Marty Wilde was lucky to be able to construct a quiff at all, having started to go bald at 13.

The greatest travesty of Elvis on stage was reserved for the King himself. His grotesquely overweight later embodiment now appears to be one of the saddest and most extreme manifestations of pop kitsch. The Fat Elvis wobbling along a Las Vegas stage, squeezed and sweating into the flared white rhinestone catsuits that he favoured, had abandoned all his charisma and sex appeal in favour of indulgence, cheeseburgers, mind-numbing cocktails of drugs and hard-core pornography. All that remained was something that resembled a distorted photograph of his younger sexy self and a slowed-down version of the famous voice. It is a comic image that is currently being exploited very successfully by a man who calls himself Tort Elvis - all gyrating over-sized hips and cantilevered quiff. Tort is not only a very funny impressionist but also the lead singer with American comic-rock cabaret act Dread Zeppelin.

MUM AND DAD'S GROOVY TUNES

Awful pop is not only produced for teenagers - much of the middle-of-the-road music that is bought by your parents or by that dying breed called housewives is a veritable treasure chest of kitsch. Family entertainers such as Barry Manilow, Val Doonican and Engelbert Humperdinck have an appeal that is the musical equivalent of a Tretchikoff picture.

With their sensible comfortable clothing styles and cheesy showbiz smiles, these artistes appear alien to the trendy world of the hit parade. Indeed, this very unfashionability forms the basis of their appeal to the kitsch devotee. Mum and Dad's musical taste is likely to be a good source of amusement, even if it is only rock wrinklies like the Rolling Stones. But it is better still when their favourite artistes are the likes of Max Bygraves and Conway Twitty whose long-faded mediocre talents never went with a swing. And paradise is yours if the dust-collecting end of their record collections harbours *Country & Western Yodelling Favourites*, *The Greatest Hits of Gene Autry*, the Singing Cowboy and Liberace.

THE PIANO-SHAPED WORLD OF LIBERACE

Liberace occupies the same high ranking in kitsch legend as Jayne Mansfield. Like Jayne, his fame far exceeded his talent, if by that you mean singing, writing and performing. But his real talent was none of these; it was a veritable genius for extravagance and publicity, which

FH 1

Kitsch kings and queen. Sexy (Engelbert Humperdinck, above), sentimental (Barry Manilow, top) and sensational (Liberace, right) or just bumptious, bland and beggaring the imagination, either way you have to hand it to these performers for having sold records and concert tickets by the zillion - and having made several hairdressers very rich.

74

means he is best remembered as a glitzy, queenie showman.

Liberace had eight homes at the last count, several in close vicinity to the glittery casinos of Las Vegas where he performed most frequently. Each of these homes was crammed with all kinds of treasures and delights - a strange mixture of antiques and junk, all chosen personally. He was an incurable collector - gold leaf, crystal and chandeliers were common to every single room of each of his abodes. The chandeliers were inescapable. Large, baroque candle-holders added their puny glow to the burning arc lights that lit every performance. Liberace's piano was never without one, icons that became more famous than his playing.

Liberace was as far removed from your secretive world-hating superstar as possible. His homes were like public exhibition halls second only to Disneyland. One Christmas an entire house was bedecked with giant decorations, music was played through massive speakers and Liberace's voice boomed out to passers-by wishing them greetings of the season. With stunts like this the house became a major attraction and he was plagued with visitors at all hours of the day and night. Although life was like living in a fishbowl for most of the time for Liberace, he revelled in parading his taste and wealth before the world. These displays were perceived by him as an act of 'sharing' his good fortune with the people who had bestowed it upon him; he was giving them a little back as a gesture of his gratitude.

Whether you regard this 'sharing' ethos as true philanthropy or as bovine excrement, he was indeed the most fabulous figure. Just as Jayne Mansfield had the pink fluffy heart as a motif, he went for the piano. His Los Angeles home (another mansion off Sunset Boulevard, formerly owned by silent film star Rudy Vallee) was dominated by piano shapes. He had piano motifs on furniture, wallpaper, rugs, everything right down to the light fittings. He also had a piano-shaped swimming pool, which he had successfully negotiated as a freebie from a pool builder on the grounds that he would benefit from the publicity that would inevitably be generated. His obsessions did not stop at keyboards: for instance, he had all the natural lawns in his garden ripped up and replaced with an astroturf carpet, and, most bizarrely of all, heaters were installed into hidden positions in the tall conifer trees that surrounded the pool so that the atmosphere outside could be heated to a minimum temperature of 70°F all year round! To cap it all, as an affirmation of his position as a king of kitsch, he was the proud owner of a Rolls Royce patriotically resprayed red, white and blue.

NOVELTY POP

The genre of comedy music boasts some particularly grotesque mutations - though the whole genre is a kitsch oddball. 'Novelty' records mostly appear to have been carefully designed to annoy the hell out of people and hold the record-buying public to ransom. Sometimes the ploy seems to be to play one relentlessly on the radio, in the shops and on TV until every available copy has been bought.

Pop cries out to be satirised, but when anybody attempts to fuse comedy with pop, instead of witty criticism all we get is a cosy, self-congratulatory humour which actually reinforces pop's bogus sentimentality and corny music. Any record by musical comedy acts such as Freddie and the Dreamers, the Barron Knights, or Weird Al Yancowicz makes the kitsch Top 100 because they so blatantly set out to dig you in the ribs that the only humour they generate is the listener's delight in their artistes' total lack of embarrassment.

Freddie and the Dreamers are remembered by most people as a kind of Beatles for four-year-olds, with Freddie never letting up in his attempts to entertain with his bespectacled goon-like persona and

Freddie of Freddie and the Dreamers is only one of many to demonstrate how pop music comedy is about as funny as pop broken hearts are genuinely tragic.

77

kangaroo jumping. The Barron Knights and Weird Al Yancowicz have enjoyed success with spoofs of the big hits of the time, but they changed the words so they were, er, funny. Yancowicz's biggest smash was a re-reading of Michael Jackson's 'Beat It', but reworked into a tale of overeating called 'Eat It' - 'have some more yoghurt, have some more pie, it doesn't matter don't be too shy, just eat it, eat it'.

Most kitsch cognoscenti extend no more than pitying tolerance to these outpourings, but deliberately bad records made by comedians in a vaguely pop idiom have a special place in their hearts. The outrageously sexist Benny Hill is a particular favourite. The words of his huge 1971 hit 'Ernie (The Fastest Milkman in the West)' inanely describe a battle of ardour between Ernie the eponymous milkman and his adversary, Two-Ton Ted, an overweight baker from Teddington, Middlesex, for the affections of one of their female customers. Sociologists have been pondering since on what it was about the record's feeble puns and boorish innuendoes that made millions of people buy it; nowadays some collectors regard it as a kitsch classic. These people also collect other irritatingly bad records by comedians of the sixties such as Charlie Drake's 'My Boomerang Won't Come Back', The Avengers' Patrick MacNee and Honor Blackman's 'Kinky Boots' and Peter Sellers' deliberately hammy 1965 spoken version of the Beatles' classic 'A Hard Day's Night'.

SINGING BY STARS WHO CAN'T

It is generally accepted that records made by football squads or any other sports personalities don't even attempt to be music, but are usually little more than oafish terrace-chants for the fans. Unfortunately, there is the odd exception when these athletes actually try to sing and make a 'proper' record. The Liverpool soccer star of the seventies, Kevin Keegan (with the band Smokie) had a Top 30 hit in the UK in 1979 with 'Head Over Heels in Love', but its success was more to do with the blind (or deaf) loyalty of the fans than its embarrassing musical shortcomings. Most football songs are more sensibly boozy and bloke-ish affairs; Paul 'Gazza' Gascoigne's reworking of the geordie anthem 'Fog on the Tyne' (1990), and the Chicago Bears 'Rap Theme' featuring their legendary colossus of a line-backer 'the Fridge' for the Superbowl, are examples.

The kitsch pleasure of watching a person promoting a pop record whilst the subtext reveals that their soul is unmistakably crying out 'I don't want to do this', is not derived purely from sportspeople. Other celebrities have willingly trapped themselves in this uncomfortable position - most frequently pop stars trying one comeback too many, but quite often TV soap stars like Richard Chamberlain singing words to the theme from Dr Kildare (1960), or Telly (Kojak) Savalas 'If' (1975). Clint Eastwood, the Man with No Name, became the Man with No Ear when he contributed 'I Sing to the Trees' to the 1970 musical western *Paint Your Wagon*. It has to be seen and not just heard, as he croons wistfully in a most untypically self-conscious manner...to trees in a wooded glade (perhaps the only fit audience)!

THE GOLDEN AGE OF ROCK'N'ROLL-GLAM ROCK

In the early seventies popular music had drifted into extremes. There was either the purportedly anti-commercial 'progressive' music that artistes such as Pink Floyd, the Doors and Jimi Hendrix had helped to establish, or the bubblegum pop which was possibly even more brainless than ever. Things were so bad that one of 1971's biggest hits was 'Chirpy Chirpy Cheep Cheep' by Middle of the Road, which told the tale of an orphaned chicklet having to cope with the uncertainty of

The Golden Age of Glitter (Gary that is).

79

the world on its own for the first time. And if this was too demanding there was the music that your parents liked, made by people like Peters and Lee, Mrs Mills and Frankie Vaughan. Or worse - the Osmonds appeared in 1972 and for years it seemed that neither they nor public taste would grow up. There was no centre ground: the Beatles were over, Elvis had gone to fat, Dylan was into drugs and weirdness, and most of the exciting sixties groups were being eclipsed by newer acts that played interminable numbers that you had to sit and listen to, such as Led Zeppelin, Yes and Fleetwood Mac. Pop, for a while, was lost. That was until they discovered glitter.

Growing out of the excesses of the sixties, glitter did not seem so strange at the time, but radical changes were in fact taking place in the pop world that meant that the entire western world would have to learn a new body language - or else trip over its trouser bottoms. 'Glamour' became the dominant force. People experimented with clothes, music, gender and drugs with an intense hedonism. The height of fashion was to look as much like the opposite sex as possible, dressed from head to foot in shiny, twinkly materials like satin, velvet and sequins, while carrying a New York Dolls album under your arm and confessing to bisexuality. Partytime was in the air, though you might not be sure of the sex of the person you left the party with.

The music that went with all this came to be known as Glam Rock, or Glitter Rock. It was essentially a mix of fifties rock'n'roll with a little dash of roaring twenties flamboyance. It was loud and rhythmically simple. But it is not the sounds that are so important in the story of kitsch as the appearance of those who made them. Singers and groups in the first half of the seventies came encased in huge outlines - shirts had to have big, usually rounded collars, hair was long or puffed up, spiky and often dyed vivid hues of orange, jet black or blue. Trousers were tight and high at the waist and long and flappy by the ankles, and shoes were stacked and platformed. Groups stood tall and appeared much larger than life. The pallid complexions of those who lived mainly by night - male and female - were brought to life by brightly coloured make up. Even ordinary people dressed as if they were going out to a wild fancy dress party for every occasion, even the office. It was a shiny, glitzy time; exotic and ostentatious fabrics such as see-through chiffon, lurex, cheesecloth and PVC were favoured. Pop stars set the trend, with ever-higher platforms and ever-growing sheets of material on their legs, and the public followed.

When set next to today's designer-influenced imagery the extreme, ambiguous and outrageous Glam Rock era couldn't be more contrary.

The pop musicians sought after by the kitsch collector of today are those who merely followed the extreme trends of their time. The smarter ones, like Marc Bolan or David Bowie (above), stayed ahead of the game, Bowie sensibly killing off his Ziggy Stardust role in 1973 even though the fans were clamouring for more. Bolan perhaps took it a bit far by getting himself killed for real.

The joke then was that the singer of one of these groups was in hospital with a broken leg, because he had fallen off his shoes. A great joke now would be to dig out the patent stars and stripes platform boots you wore as a teenager and have them mounted in a glass display case for the front room, or better still to wear them the next time you have guests around for a sophisticated dinner party. To round it off why not put on a Bay City Rollers album as well?

Glam Rock was quite simply pop to be enjoyed purely for fun, in contrast to the imponderable seriousness of the bombed-out supergroups you couldn't even tap your fingers to. But to the post-style revolution eyes of the 1990s, the likes of groups such as Wizzard, Mud, Alice Cooper and the Sweet unself-consciously blitzing ballrooms and dancing tiger feet seem so cumbersome, awkward and sensationally unattractive they are comic. The problem is not that music was meant to be fun, but its rhythmic and melodic crudeness, allied to a self-conscious 'aren't we enjoying ourselves' attitude.

The further down the ladder of success you go the tackier the kitsch to be found. If you have the wish to find something a little more esoteric in terms of Glam or Glitter Rock, artistes like David Bowie and Marc Bolan (and Elton John - but more on him in 'Fashion') were serious musicians who were the style leaders of their day but who managed to produce some good music as well. If their past selves appear to look silly today, at least they moved on and changed with the times (in Bowie's case, legend always has him a little ahead of them). One-hit wonders such as Kenny, Chicory Tip and Flintlock on the other hand are much more worth seeking out because they lacked the wit to see beyond the extremities of fashion - and oh, let's face it, they were pretty ugly and spotty with it.

NEW ROMANTICS

In the early eighties, the last freak-out before the style lords assumed control of design and lifestyle starred an androgynous club-based bunch of musical cultists called New Romantics. Although glamour and hedonism were again on the menu, this was not quite the free-for-all of a decade earlier. Musically, the 'electronic' revolution replaced guitars with synthesizers. Sartorially, men wore costumes inspired by romantic figures from history such as Robin Hood and Don Juan. They refused to smile, but had begun to wear make-up again.

Photographic evidence reveals that artistes like Spandau Ballet, Duran Duran, Modern Romance and Steve Strange have the potential to be accorded the same kitsch status as their Glam Rock ancestors. All

One of the appeals of bad old pop music is nostalgia. But nostalgia for the early seventies, and groups like The Glitter Band?

that is needed is time. They already look daft, with their peek-a-boo fringe hairstyles, flowing robes and 'Aladdin' trousers tucked into pixie boots. But worse than their precious flamboyance was the way that many of these groups made serious claims about changing the world through their music. They spoke of New Romanticism as a new art movement or philosophy, which in a severe economic recession offered people the opportunity of aesthetic escapism. Pretentious, moi?

The New Romantics of the early eighties like Steve Strange hoped to bring beauty and sensitivity back into rock music, but ended up looking, and sometimes sounding, as if they had been with Dorothy in *The Wizard of Oz*.

POP WILL EAT ITSELF

The difficulty with Glam Rock is that you never know quite how seriously you are meant to take it. However, more recent times have seen the appearance of several groups with a more systematic approach to pop kitsch. Glasgow's Rez(v)illos, New York's the Ramones, Atlanta's B52s and London's Bananarama have all lampooned the brightly-coloured throwaway nature of pop. The musicians of these groups have keen eyes and ears for the bubblegum pop of the fifties and sixties. They have taken the comic-strip appearance of bands like Jan and Dean, the Beach Boys and the Monkees and mimicked the nostalgic appeal of the original record sleeves. They have used their music as an inspiration to create packages of highly visual but danceable pop for today's kitsch-conscious audience.

On top of this, several musical acts have successfully managed to create highly saleable pop music while at the same time poking fun at both the exploitative and bogus nature of the music business and at the consumer for being fooled by it. Sigue Sigue Sputnik, Devo and Pet Shop Boys have all achieved this double act without apparently causing offence to either record companies or the record-buying public.

Being children of the fifties and sixties, the members of these bands had already spent a lifetime studying and absorbing the phoniness and the meaninglessness of pop music culture. They have then recreated its features, tongue very much in cheek, and dressed it all up as epic anthemic pop and rock for a fresh generation of unaware teenies. Meanwhile, a more sophisticated older crowd liked them because they shared the joke. Taking things to the extreme, in the late seventies Devo argued for the de-evolution of the human race. They claimed that the rediscovery of our primitive ancestors' values was the only way to preserve a future for our species. At the same time they wore upturned flower pots on their heads and knocked out very catchy bubblegum-rock ('Whip It' was a number one hit in the USA in 1980). This, you could say, is indicative of a bunch of guys with a sense of humour about what they do.

Pet Shop Boy Neil Tennant showed his appreciation of the heart-felt values of pop when he sang, 'When I get back to my own small flat, I want to hear somebody bark', ('I Want A Dog', 1987). He did so confident in the knowledge that half of the group's hordes of fans don't listen to the lyrics and are blissfully unaware that the mickey is being taken as they bop away to the electronic dance backdrop. All in all, the Pet Shop Boys play the parts of anti-pop stars very well. They are the Gilbert and George of the pop world, indistinct personalities who are

Subtly exposing the kitsch superficialities of the pop world, the Pet Shop Boys' lyrics on songs like 'I Want a Dog' and 'Let's Make Lots of Money' are a deliberate banal joke. They are written in the full knowledge that none of the fans listen to the lyrics, bliissfully unaware that the mickey is being taken as they bop away to the electronic dance backdrop.

extremely polite when interviewed and who don't smile for photographs.

Possibly the ultimate spoof pop act was Sigue Sigue Sputnik. They guyed the cult of outrage and shock that has been popular since Elvis's hips first wiggled so menacingly in the fifties. They camped things up to androgynous extremes, and revelled in the fact that nothing they did was original - their music certainly wasn't, as they had 'sampled' the vast majority of it. Finally, they hyped their own value by falsely claiming an $8 million recording contract advance, which would have been one of the largest in history. The music was pretty inconsequential but they caught the public's eye because of their hairstyles and costumes and their excellent take-offs of the pretentions of the promo videos of the mid-eighties. Unfortunately, the little bubble they created popped quite suddenly when the public discovered that EMI had really given them a modest $150,000. The public, clearly, did not see the joke.

OUT OF SIGHT

The music video was the most powerful promotional tool of the music industry of the eighties. Videos were popular with TV companies because they were supplied free of charge by the record companies, and so represented an exceptionally cheap source of programming. They were popular with record companies because they were much, much cheaper to make than TV commercials, plus they didn't have to pay to have them screened. They were popular with the public because they were a new way to experience and enjoy music.

However, it soon transpired that the fund of ideas available to illustrate a pop song was severely limited. What was hailed in the early eighties as a new and exciting art form quickly descended into the same empty bathos that fatally taints the rest of the pop industry. Form, as so often, triumphed over substance. Girls getting out of cars wearing impossibly short skirts, lonely girls and guys peering through windows for long-lost loves, clumsy dance routines enhanced by a perpetually moving camera, heavy metal bands performing on sets that look like fire escapes (with a half-dressed girl in dream sequence) - these are just a sample of the vacuous and much-repeated imagery that was used to sell more pop.

Such videos are still made, but TV stations are no longer excited by them, and, more importantly, it seems that the public has become bored with them, too. The much-hailed revolution of music video through satellite and cable television has simply not materialised and kids have started to go to clubs again, a lot of bands make their own videos, and record companies are at last questioning their effectiveness as marketing ploys and are making severe cutbacks in their production. But if you enjoyed them, don't worry. The originals will soon be back on the circuit again, when we will marvel at their pretentiousness.

AND STILL THE MUSIC GOES ROUND

Kitsch in music, possibly more than in any other area, is thrown up primarily by rapid changes in fashion. As we have seen, the music world is a fickle and fast-changing one where within just a matter of months the hippest latest new idea can seem as out-dated and as naff as something 20 years old. So with this and the highly subjective nature of the subject, you can easily find your favourite type of kitsch music. You could try the bump'n'grind and tacky sleaze of seventies disco - all those white satin flared suits and flamboyant macho dance routines. Or perhaps the entire brash and brutal Heavy Metal circus with its male-dominated sexography. Or the guileless bobby-sox love songs of the early sixties. The field is wide open because bad taste and pop go together like stylus and groove. Anything can be enjoyed as kitsch if you can laugh while you listen. Don't worry if the kitsch of past music is too familiar still to thrill you. Somewhere, in the hyper-sophisticated, multi-track, digitized recording studios of the Western world new kitsch is being manufactured at this very minute. Remember the Christmas single from 1990's pop phenomenon, New Kids on the Block? Well, if you can't, don't worry, most people couldn't remember it by New Year's Eve. Just look in the current Top Ten instead; I guarantee you won't be disappointed.

MONEY FOR GOD'S SAKE

THE HIGHBROW

The highbrow society of the art world actually numbers very few people, but they constitute an extremely influential crowd. Just like the cognoscenti who originally defined the concept of taste at the end of the seventeenth century, this small elite of artists, art historians, critics, gallery-owners and museum directors spend their time debating aesthetic virtues, usually with well-articulated politeness. However, this erudite chatter is not confined now to salons or to private viewings at art galleries and auction rooms. For today's cognoscenti enjoy the great privilege of having their thoughts and theories aired in the columns of art journals, newspapers and the plethora of television and radio arts programmes. But sadly possession of the sense of humour which is essential to appreciate kitsch debars anyone from joining their company.

The art establishment's attitude towards kitsch has changed little since the term was invented, despite the mutations in the public's view of it since the early seventies. For these intellectuals to celebrate kitsch is beyond their comprehension. Isn't it associated with nasty, brutish lowbrow popular culture?

ANTI-ART (PART ONE)

To have good taste is pretty pointless unless it confers some sort of prestige upon the owner, and so the effect of the pronouncements of

Shaun Clarkson (pictured opposite relaxing at home surrounded by his work) is an artist/designer who takes ordinary domestic objects from whisks to irons and embellishes them with glitter and costume jewelry, turning the ordinary into the hyperordinary. The surreal edge to his sense of humour, as in this Nancy Reagan teapot, revels in the millions of mass-produced objects that are similarly decorated.

87

those people who possess such boundless quantities of it has been to put art itself on a pinnacle. However, this doesn't always go down too well with the people who actually produce the stuff. As the art establishment has become more and more established, so there have also been more groups of artists who reject their patronage as, well, patronising. As a command of French is de rigueur for any art pundit, so these unruly artists are also termed in French, the avant-garde.

One of the most significant groups of the early twentieth century avant-garde was a bunch of artists who met in the neutral state of Switzerland, having fled there at the outbreak of the First World War. Having little truck with the war and the culture that caused it, they launched a ferocious assault on the art and aesthetic values of the time. They were one of the first art movements to identify themselves as such and give themselves a name - Dada. The word had no meaning, but sounded babyish. It was deliberately anti-art, chosen to reflect their philosophy that art had become a pompous old dinosaur that made sense to very few people.

Dadaists were the punk rockers of the art world. They aimed to topple art from its previously exclusive pedestal. By conducting guerilla warfare on the bourgeoisie and the art establishment, they hoped to convince the public that it need no longer be down to the nobs to define art and good taste.

One of the best known Dadaists, Marcel Duchamp, set out to cause an almighty outrage in the art world when he exhibited a common-or-garden wine rack he'd bought from a New York store in 1914. It worked, and he provoked a huge outcry. In 1917 he went a stage further, when in a wonderfully befitting gesture of disdain for the status quo, he chose to enter a urinal (signed by R. Mutt) for an international exhibition of new art.

Through the use of such 'objets trouvés', Duchamp and the other Dadaists were pretty effective in their efforts to make people look at art through fresh eyes. The urinals, wine racks and coat stands they exhibited were all self-evidently mundane, and to pretend they were art was even worse than outrageous; it was in the worst possible taste. They challenged 'art' by accusing it of being kitsch, implying that the good taste that it represented was totally false. Art was supposed to be ennobling, edifying, the finest expression of the human spirit, but all these wonderful values had led to the pointless slaughter of millions on the battlefields of Belgium and Northern France. Dadaists considered the mainstream culture of the early twentieth century was itself kitsch - the product of a supposedly high-minded set of values that delivered

At an exhibition of new art in 1917 the Dadaist Marcel Duchamp showed what he thought of the art world by exhibiting this ordinary urinal. It had the desired effect; the art world was suitably horrified, but it had the last laugh as the urinal itself has now become widely recognised as 'art'.

miserably less than it promised. Duchamp's implicit statement was that an oil painting with a high price tag was no more worthy of consideration than a urinal - maybe less so.

But, by one of those comic twists that the history of kitsch loves, Duchamp's everyday objects have now become 'art' as well. His urinal and wine rack have been painstakingly photographed and exquisitely reproduced in many an expensive art book. And, as we've said, the art cognoscenti does not have a sense of humour.

A PORTRAIT OF THE ARTIST AS A CON MAN (PART ONE)

The acceptance, drainage and disinfection of Duchamp's lavatorial creations by the art establishment is but one example of its infuriating ability to pull the rug from under the feet of its critics. The trick was repeated many times on Dada's successors.

The energy and philosophy of the Dadaists was part of a much-wider movement for change. It was one bit in a massive re-thinking process of all the arts, from music to painting and architecture. One movement that came out of this was Surrealism, which was launched in 1919 by a French artist, André Breton. The Surrealists aimed to express the subconscious mind by using images that occur in dreams, and in putting together startling combinations of everyday objects.

Regarded by fellow Surrealists as an old poser, Salvador Dali knew how to paint what the public would buy. This extravagant showman avoided all questions about whether what he was producing was really art by giving enigmatic and obscure replies that might just be taken as profound.

There was, however, a joker in the pack among the group. Salvador Dali became the best known Surrealist of them all, because he sold the most reproductions (posters of his paintings were particularly popular on university campus walls in the seventies). His fans argue that he attempted to illustrate the twentieth-century psyche in terms of the vocabulary of everyday life. Believe that if you wish; others say that his iconography of melting watches, telephones, fried eggs, shapes in sand dunes and amorphous noses was glib and empty. Certainly, nobody has ever given a satisfactory explanation of these symbols, the normal defence being to cop out in the claim that they are 'beyond mere explanation'. Enter witness for the prosecution - Dali himself: 'The famous soft watches are nothing else but the tender, extravagant, paranoiac-critical Camembert of time space.'

One thing you had to hand to Dali was that he was a flamboyant and colourful personality, a fabulous enigma much loved by the media. This caused him to overshadow and subsequently annoy the more serious Surrealists, who reviled him as an old poser. Breton disowned him, as he considered his work vulgar because of its popularity, and used to refer to him by the apt anagram of his name, 'Avida Dollars'.

Dali's hallucinatory images were well-painted, blending the elegance of Renaissance painting styles with a vivid naturalism. But clever as they are, they are essentially phony and meaningless, a perfect definition of kitsch. Like all kitsch merchants, Dali was motivated to make more and more money from people who thought they were buying something of value. In this case, if they couldn't read a meaning into any of his pictures, they considered themselves to be ever-so-clever in owning one. When questioned on this subject in 1968, Dali replied with a typical pretence of being enigmatic, 'It is not necessary for the public to know whether I am joking or whether I am serious, just as it is not necessary for me to know it myself.'

Of course, there is much more art of highly dubious value that changes hands at auctions and galleries the world over for ludicrously high prices. Much loved by the smart in the early seventies were the Symbolist painters of nearly 100 years previously. In many ways Dali's forebears, they set out to create images of the world as a happy balance between man, nature and the heavens, especially the group's best known painters Gustav Moreau and Pierre Puvis de Chavannes. Moreau's attempts to fuse the spiritual and physical worlds produced the most vacuous quasi-religious imagery, with godesses, angels and Christ-like apparitions appearing in most of his canvases. Typical of these is possibly his best-known picture 'Galatea' (1880-81), where the head of John the Baptist can be seen floating unsupported in mid-air gazing with a loving intensity at an unaware sleeping beauty. The beauty is, naturally, nude, except for knee-length blonde tresses and

The portentous imagery of the Symbolists of the late nineteenth century came back into vogue in the 1970s. In the canvases of Gustave Moreau (above – 'Galatée') and Puvis de Chavannes (left – 'St John the Baptist'), man's quest for peace and harmony was expressed in mystical terms, but somehow a strong and quite unethereal sensuality would manage to force its way on to the canvas through the other-worldliness.

Pop Artists of the sixties pushed the boundaries of art outwards by integrating commercial imagery into their work. Anything from comic books (right – Roy Lichtenstein 'In the Car, fur' to food labels (below - Andy Warhol, 'Campbell's Soup Can') became a fit subject for art. There is nothing necessarily kitsch about a banana or a soup can, but by trawling commercial imagery so widely, Pop artists sometimes caught kitsch in their nets.

crown of flowers matching the seat of flowers she reclines on, probably as a representation of nature itself. Puvis de Chavannes' pictures often depict naked nymphets and pixie-like creatures bathing in magical lakes in idyllic summer bucolic settings.

Less exotic, but equally often banal art remains with us in countless official portraits, extravagant avant-garde theories and pallid imitations of defunct art movements. One of the best places to go and enjoy these now is the annual summer exhibition at London's Royal Academy, where several galleries are turned over to a year's creations of mainly second-hand ideas.

ANTI-ART (PART TWO)

Dada laid the way for various subsequent artists to challenge ruling notions of good art, but it was not until several decades later that the questions of art and kitsch, the highbrow and the lowbrow in culture were raised again in a challenging manner. The Pop artists of the late fifties and the sixties forced the issue of popular culture on to the agenda of the art world. Andy Warhol, Roy Lichtenstein, Robert Rauschenberg, Jasper Johns and Claes Oldenberg in the USA and Richard Hamilton and Peter Blake in the UK, associated by friendship, locations and shared exhibitions, scandalised much of the art establishment by choosing subjects from 'bad' or commercialised art. They painted what they had been educated to despise - some of it kitsch, and all of it quite far beyond the palette as far as dominant ideas of art were concerned.

They appeared on the scene in a complacent and materialistic era. The British Prime Minister Harold Macmillan told the population that they'd never had it so good, and throughout the Western world the rapidly spreading media had become crammed full of signs and messages goading the public with ways of spending their ever-increasing disposable incomes. Pop artists simply took from features of what was for most people their real daily visual landscape and fashioned them into new subjects for art.

These artists were fascinated by the product logos and packaging of commonplace everyday groceries such as Coca-Cola bottles, soup cans and the other goods that now proliferated on supermarket shelves. The superstars of the movie and pop music world like Marilyn Monroe, Elvis Presley and the Beatles were seen to have become further commercial objects; their powerful public images were stripped of personality in having become something else to buy. In Pop Art,

Peter Blake, 'Got A Girl'. Pop Artists saw that the superstars of the movie and pop world were treated as commodities just like baked beans and washing powder.

entertainers and soft drinks inhabited the same cultural universe as comic books, neon advertising and strident newspaper headlines.

Predictably, Pop artists were initially reviled by the establishment. In 1966 Roy Lichtenstein was condemned by *Life* magazine as 'the worst artist in the US'. This didn't worry him as he freely admitted that he chose to create paintings which were large blown-up details of popular comic strips precisely because they would get up the noses of the establishment. Warhol antagonised the precious sensibilities of the art world even further. He rarely had any physical contact with the works of art that bore his signature, but preferred to consider himself as a sort of art version of an industrial magnate, employing a staff in a 'factory' that produced works of art to his designs and orders. All of this was far removed from the conventionally held and romanticised vision of an artist, working solo, often in poverty, with oil paint and canvas, watercolours and parchment or bronze or plaster.

Moreover, it was bad enough that massive and gaudily colourful images of everyday goods and movie stars and large comic book blow-ups had come along just after the art historians and genteel critics had come to terms with Abstract Expressionism and the other abstractions. But even greater offence was caused by the fact that the cheap reproductions of the work of Warhol, Lichtenstein, Blake and Hamilton were finding their way into people's front rooms with incredible ease and rapidity. These artists were commercially in tune with the middle classes in the way that Tretchikoff was simultaneously engaging the lower classes. At least Rembrandt and Constable had had the good taste to die before their works were mass-produced.

Pop Art successfully pointed out that we are surrounded almost everywhere by graphics and visual symbols, some of which are kitsch, but that we don't even notice them, so numbed are we by the massive exposure we endure to commercial imagery from birth. Equally importantly, it also underlined the fact that these same elements have an undeniable charm all of their own - which when used out of the context can be translated into a work of art.

A PORTRAIT OF THE ARTIST AS A CON MAN (PART TWO)

Pop Art is not, of course, concerned solely, or even mainly with kitsch. Of greater significance here than its occasional use of kitsch objects is that Pop turned its back on traditional art subjects by saying that modern mass-produced objects were more interesting. It thereby opened the door for art into the Garden of Earthly Kitsch, creating a threshold that has been happily trodden by several artists since.

Jeff Koons is currently considered to be America's premier bad-boy artist. He began his career as a salesman selling memberships for the Museum of Modern Art in New York. It wasn't long before Wall Street wooed him with the prospect of higher wages as a commodities broker, which the then-aspiring artist claimed he needed in order to produce the sculptures that were costing him $3,000 each. It was clearly a profound experience, for the absurdity of trading pork bellies from a computer screen in downtown Manhattan was to find itself reincarnated in Koons' sculpture. For example, his 'The New' collection of 1988 showed brand new vacuum cleaners encased in perspex.

But Koons' pertinence to kitsch and hence his appearance here in these pages begins with his first major exhibition, 'Banality' in 1989-90, which was held simultaneously at galleries in New York, Chicago and Munich. The show consisted of porcelain and polychromed wood

Jeff Koons' sculpture emulates the world of mail-order ornamental middle American kitsch, only he inflates it to massive proportions to emphasise its garishness. Porcelain and polychromed sculptures such as this one of Michael Jackson with his pet chimpanzee Bubbles looks as though it could fit comfortably onto your mantelpiece at home, but is in fact not far short of lifesize.

sculptures made to Koons' instructions by Italian and German craftsmen (the new artist rarely gets his hands dirty). The sculptures ran the whole gamut of cultural icons from John the Baptist to Michael Jackson, rendered to look like over-sized airport gift shop souvenirs or mammoth 3-D renderings of the cartoon characters that have ruled the imaginations of TV-raised Americans.

Among the more provocative pieces were a dimpled Italian love-me bear sporting an insidiously vacuous expression; a heart-shaped button and a pot of gingham-covered jam; a topless Playboy blonde embracing a limp-limbed Pink Panther whose sad, yellow eyes reveal an unspeakable despair; and the pièce de resistance, a huge larger-than-life sculpture of a gilded and white-faced Michael Jackson cuddling Bubbles, his scarily similarly-featured pet chimpanzee!

This is the souvenir-stand and mail-order ornamental kitsch of

'Ilona on Top' - one of Koons' porno-kitsch paintings of himself with Italian porn-star-turned-politician, Cicciolina. Success in his artistic aim was achieved when someone slashed these canvases at the Venice Biennale.

middle America enlarged to massive proportions to emphasise all of its lurid awfulness. Koons' sculpture emulates this tasteless, vulgar and dumb world - laying bare the ugliest, most banal side of modern life. His work packs an emotional wallop that raises unsettling questions about what art is supposed to be. Much to the satisfaction of Koons the businessman, the 'Banality' sculptures brought in loads of cash, making him a multi-millionaire and one of the richest contemporary artists.

Koons has continued to shock and offend, bashing away at the frontiers of what is perceived to be good and bad taste. He now claims to be in love with Cicciolina, née Illona Staller - the Italian porn star who made the headlines when she was elected to the Italian parliament, and who in 1990 offered to let Saddam Hussein 'rape' her if he freed the Western hostages he was holding in Iraq prior to the war. Koons says of her 'She is one of the greatest artists in the world - instead of painting or photography, she articulates her genitalia!'

Koons and Cicciolina have been exploring what can only be described as porno-kitsch. One succès de scandale was at the 1990 Venice Biennale, the art world's Cannes Festival, where he exhibited a polychromed sculpture of Cicciolina and himself as a soft-core Adam and Eve in the Garden of Eden, surrounded by three large and explicit laser-painted and varnished pictures of the couple making love. It was so successful in being provocative that one fanatic slashed each painting with a knife.

One of the tackiest and most extreme forms of kitsch is pornography - the ultimate in the seductive promise that always fails to deliver. Koons seized on this in his hyper-real pictures, featuring such tender and intimate moments as his performing oral sex on Cicciolina as she stuffs a glass dildo into her freshly-shaven vagina. Koons next sought to give his work with Cicciolina mass appeal by making a film, *Made in Heaven*, which he was to produce, direct and star in himself, with the guarantee of lots of explicit sex.

Koons is considered by many in the art world to be a genius for daring to push at the limits of acceptability in art, but there is the ambivalent morality of a no-nonsense hard-nosed businessman evident in all of his thoughts and work. He is considered by many others to be a charlatan, a suspicion raised in people's minds because of his public image. For media interviews he usually wears the sharp suits and tab-collars of his former incarnation as a Wall Street trader, and adopts a cool and calculating business-speak when discussing art and himself. This could be (and probably is) a deliberate ploy to alienate the art establishment further, with the bonus that it adds entertainment value to his marketability as an international artist. Koons' work reflects the view that if kitsch is an acceptable aesthetic, then art should celebrate, explore and question it just like any other aesthetic value. He says, 'The art world has never had to deal with the populist level - I don't think that's correct. High art to me is just ineffective art - art that can't get an audience. Madonna has been on the cover of every major magazine. That's impact.'

DESIGNER KITSCH: GRAPHICS

Pierre et Gilles are two French art photographers and image-makers who create a technicolor paradise that rarely fails to enchant all who fall under its spell. Their work is a cornucopia of junky imagery of popular culture from all over the world, with a strong emphasis on religion and mythology. Jesus, Hindu gods, angels and characters from assorted fairy tales and worldwide mythologies throng their work quite indiscriminately.

Pierre et Gilles create a heavily stylised portraiture which has won them the status of darlings of the pop and fashion media, where they are sought after to make book covers, record sleeves and pop videos. Boy George commissioned a portrait from them in 1990 and was transmogrified into a glittering pipe-playing Indian god. On the LP sleeve they designed for Marc Almond's 'A Lover Spurned', Almond disports himself with a mermaid. When Jean-Paul Gaultier wanted something for the cover of his comic-strip autobiography, *A Nous Deux la Mode*, Pierre et Gilles gave him with a winsome, child-like smile and portrayed him clutching a posy of daisies against an idyllic tourist-view of Paris au printemps.

The two French artist-designers, Pierre et Gilles, pursue kitsch with an awesome enthusiasm. They produce portraits and designs for record sleeves and book jackets that are set in a fantastic realm of popular religious and mythological symbolism.

Although it is self-evident that Pierre et Gilles pursue kitsch with an awesome enthusiasm, they are somewhat wary of using the term. 'We only dislike it because of the way it is used. If you say, "Wow, it's kitsch," like "Oh it's really great," then we don't mind. But most of the time it's used by the bourgeois to denigrate popular culture.' You can't get a clearer statement of the current status of kitsch than that.

Pierre et Gilles started their artistic collaboration in Paris in 1977, a year after they first met. At the time Gilles worked as a painter and Pierre as a photographer - what made them different was the decision to pool the two arts. A Pierre et Gilles piece starts with Pierre taking a photograph, which Gilles then painstakingly reworks. The results have a heightened sense of reality to them, looking like a photograph taken of the dream world. Kitsch stalks the style, not just the subject, as the resulting images are redolent of Hollywood cartoons, Indian film

posters and the illustrations in an old-fashioned family Bible.

Nothing more typifies their work than a book they created called *L'Odyssée Imaginaire*. In it they conjured forth a fantasy world populated by figures whose major sources of inspiration appear to be the super-cute paintings of big-eyed children that you can buy at newsagents and souvenir postcard stands the world over. Once again, the style recalls the intense colours and heroic poses of Indian movie posters and the unreal glossy type of portraiture that is widely used for saints, royalty and Hollywood. Nearly all the models featured are their friends - people who have achieved fame and fortune in the fashionable world of the media and art.

DESIGNER KITSCH: FURNITURE

At the very top end of furniture design, where desks and chairs are considered to be (and are as expensive as) sculpture, dwells one of the most potent manifestations of kitsch-influenced contemporary design.

Soon after its founding in 1981 under the leadership of Italian architect (and former Olivetti industrial designer), Ettore Sotsass Jr, the Memphis design group had become the most significant force in international furniture design. For six years they tackled all kinds of household objects, from vases to lighting, from office interiors and furniture to the bedroom, bathroom and toilet, from toys and pencil cases to clocks, from beds, sofas and chests of drawers to ceramics, glass and silverware. Then like some rock supergroup, which in many ways they resembled, in 1987 they split up while still on top, to pursue (or resume) individual careers. Sotsass, Allessandro Mendini, Michele de Lucchi, Matteo Thun, Aldo Cibic, Marco Zanini and the others went their separate ways, but still playing the same style of design.

You could be forgiven if your first impressions of Memphis artefacts were to check if you were still wearing your goggles from your early morning swim. The creations of this Milan-based design group have a very 'alien' edge, with skewed forms and clashing colours. Yet despite their unusual hues, patterns and materials they do bear some resemblance to conventional furniture. A multi-coloured and patterned pyramidical tower serves as a chest of drawers, a thick solid circular marble-topped tablet seated upon fibre glass feet serves as a coffee table. Memphis group designers use colour audaciously with obscenely creamy pastels of the classic fifties variety. They intentionally combine ugly tans, brilliant acid greens and glittery reds and blues. This almost visually anarchic approach to design extends most spectacularly to their materials. Their favourite surfaces are gaudily patterned plastic laminates - the sort of speckled flake metal finish that is more at home on accordions or early sixties electric guitars - which they apply onto everything from shelving units to clockfaces.

The group's design philosophy was made explicit by the radical design group they grew out of, Studio Alchymia formed in the late seventies. Sotsass and Mendini, founders of Memphis, were members. With a deliberate irony Alchymia named its first two collections 'Bauhaus 1' and 'Bauhaus 2'. In fact, these contained brightly coloured, odd-shaped furniture in complete contrast to the Bauhaus principles of rigid adherence to function and absence of decoration. The collection names were meant as a rude gesture to the dominant movement of the previous 50 years.

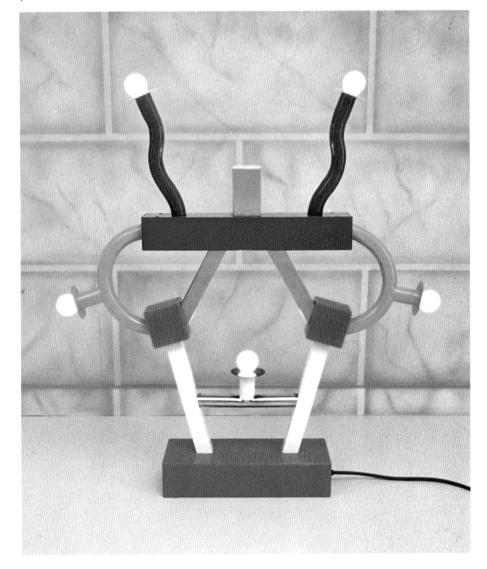

Ashoka by Ettore Sotsass. This weird-looking object of 1981 is, believe it or not, a table lamp (in painted metal). It is a classic example of the designs of the Milan-based Memphis design group that Sotsass headed. One of the most potent purveyors of kitsch-influenced contemporary design, this group of designers worked at the top end of furniture design where tables and chairs are perceived as (and are as expensive as) sculpture.

asablanca (1981) by Ettore Sotsass: a sideboard in plastic laminate with internal shelves. The name 'Memphis' reputedly originates from Bob Dylan's song, 'Memphis Blues Again', but it also conjures up both the commercialised birthplace of Elvis Presley and the ancient capital of Egypt - a juxtaposition of the ancient, the exotic, the popular and the banal that characterises the group's style.

Memphis designers were bored with the reductionist ethic of the art of the understatement in which furniture had to be cool and clean lined, pattern- and decor-less, primarily functional but also deadly serious and boring (remember the black boxes?). There had to be more to life than this, thought Sotsass, and he set out to prove this with a vengeance.

The Memphis designers are crack semioticians; they know how

people 'read' certain materials, such as how marble indicates power and wealth. Just as marble is immediately associated with 'high' class, so plastic laminates and garish colours are perceived as signs of the supposedly tacky popular taste (or all that the masses can afford). Idealistic and abstract as it may sound, Memphis mixed all these contradictory high- and low-class elements in their designs because they wished to do away with hierarchies of good and bad taste. Kitsch is scrambled with the good taste to the point where you cannot tell which material is 'high' and which is 'low'. A single piece of furniture may feature a costly and unusual wood combined with chrome, gaudy plastic laminate and coloured light bulbs. A paradox arises here, though, because even when made out of inexpensive materials like plastic laminate, Memphis furniture remains handcrafted and unique, and therefore expensive to make. Subsequently it is very, very expensive and this signifies status. Ah, another infuriating paradox from the history of kitsch? Or is this use of supposedly cheap

materials by an intellectual set of classy Italian designers itself another form of kitsch?

However, as the designers who formed Memphis widen their influence and move towards large-scale production of at least some of their pieces, prices are beginning to come down. Perhaps all this instant kitsch will soon be affordable to those who already have fifties cocktail cabinets bought for a few shekels in some junk shop.

This baby's rattle is actually a teapot ('Colorado',1983) by Marco Zanini. Memphis designers used nursery or fifties colours - either fixing on pastels or combining ugly tans with brilliant acid greens and glittery magentas and cyans.

UNDER THE CATWALK

Watch out, this could happen to you.

The scene is a party, some time in the early eighties. Everyone is dressed for the occasion, completely without inhibition, and in the very choicest numbers from their wardrobe. The door opens and in walks a

figure. He too has made a special effort. He is wearing a huge-collared summer shirt, with rounded collar, which could not be described so much as garish as a veritable spew of yellow, red and orange swirling lines. His pants, described at the time of purchase as 'slacks' are of imitation-worsted 'crimplene', chocolate brown in colour, and slightly flared at the bottoms. Below them is a pair of bright white terry-towelling socks partially encased in a pair of open-toed 'Jesus-boot' sandals. The total ensemble is an affront to the eye, the brain and the harmonic combinations of Creation. But the amazing thing is that nobody pays any attention! For this is a bad taste fancy dress party.

Fur coats, 'made of various felines'. Not so much a pride of lions as a line of prats. It is not just the clothes themselves in high fashion that look so ridiculous, but the 'arty' and pretentious way in which they are presented.

On display are over 60 different articulations of the concept of bad taste. Murder is repeatedly committed on elegance as people have chosen to wear the clashing, the overstated and the woefully out-of-fashion all at once. It is February in the middle of town, but people are wearing Hawaiian shirts and shorts; it is the eighties but others are wearing high waists, tank-tops, matching shirts, kipper ties and bell-bottoms. The darkness of the winter night is rent by the acidic hues of day-glo green, orange and pink, and the urban jungle has become the lair of fake-fur tiger, cheetah and leopard skins. The more blatant wear

104

shiny PVC, satin, lurex, crushed velvet, rubberwear or privately purchased lingerie, while those who love their firesides have come in pink fluffy slippers, hair-curlers and candlewick bathrobes.

The joy of an occasion such as this is that nobody has recourse to the theatrical costumier or the joke shop. All these garments were produced for ordinary people like you and me to wear - to work, to the cinema or slopping about at home. OK, so some of the guests go a weeny bit over the top with their combinations but everything that is

Elsa Schiaparelli's designs have long been revered by those who know about such things as imaginative and iconoclastic, but in reality she bears a heavy burden of responsibility for much that followed. These dancing circus horses might have come straight from a knitted lavatory paper holder, while even the badge mania of today (a source for future kitsch collectors) has scarcely caught up with the trapeze-artist buttons.

worn at these parties was produced because somebody, somewhere, at sometime thought it looked nice, flattering or even exciting.

COUTURE FROM HIGH TO LOW

What people most immediately think of as bad taste clothing relies on the staple kitsch criteria that defines bad taste in other areas. The objects in question are either so out of date that they have taken on a new, comic meaning (two-tone split-knee loon pants and eight-inch platform soles), are cheap and tacky imitations of expensive and exclusive original materials and designs (brushed fur cowhide), have always appeared to be outlandishly peculiar (e.g. see-through plastic trousers), or are the things that your Mom and Dad wear while listening to Jim Reeves or watching the big game on TV (fluffy slippers. cardigans with shiny buttons).

The best sources to look for clothes for bad-taste parties are second-hand stores, charity shops, elderly relatives' wardrobes or that old case on top of the cupboard where you put away some things ten years ago. But these garments have not become kitsch by virtue of their consignment to these museums of the recent past. The fashion world is a constant bubbling source of it.

All the items you might parade to amuse your friends derive at only one or two generations' removal from some couturier's drawing

These Karl Lagerfeld models (right) obviously did not realise that they could have asked the restaurant for a doggy bag. However, the model above has found the best way of keeping her dignity in a Paul Galliano outfit: purdah-style anonymity.

It is not surprising that the model looks so miserable; she has to wear this Thierry Mugler concoction. However, the very rich who actually buy couturier clothes are such victims of their deluded self-image that they look rather proud of the outfits when they wear them.

board. For example, see-through plastic trousers originated with the space-age designs of chic sixties fashion guru Courrèges. Ralph Lauren, amongst others, gave us the brightly knitted top and non-matching full length skirt. The grandparent of large and angular shapes is Elsa Schiaparelli. Schiaparelli actually had a lot to answer for: one of her outfits had small mirrors going up the front, others featured buttons shaped like bunches of flowers, smiling faces or lamb chops, and she thought nothing of mixing a prune colour with a pinkish magenta.

People's tastes change over years, decades even, but the fashion world likes us to do this with much greater frequency - seasonally, monthly, even. Shop window displays, cat-walk parades and magazine spreads are the high-pressure sales techniques designed to pull this off, bullying the poor consumer into buying more clothes or running the risk of appearing unfashionable.

But fashion is not just a simple conspiracy to seduce us into unnecessary expenditure, it can be a potent source of pleasure; if you feel good about the way you look and feel more confident with yourself, you should be better disposed to deal with the outside world. However, there are a great many people who fall prey to the pressures of fashion culture and become 'victims' of the attractive notions of idealised beauty and glamour that it promotes. These fashion victims become walking, talking kitsch when they allow their obsession with fashion to override their physical limitations. They will squeeze themselves into dresses that are too tight or too short, proudly don shirts several generations too young, or blend an array of designer-labelled patterns so clashing and garish that sunglasses need to be handed out to anyone they come into contact with. A sadist might invite one to a bad taste party without letting on.

The fashion world fools a great many people. It operates on the 'Emperor's new clothes' principle, that is, if you are told by certain people that a particular mode of dressing is the way you should look, and you seek their acceptance desperately enough and want to join their elite, then you'll believe anything they say, and wear whatever they tell you to (even if you can't afford it).

The fashion world, like the art world, is still dominated by an elite, but now, of course, their power is much more widespread than the limited regal circles of old. Today, the fashion mafiosi receive massive media coverage, in countless magazines and TV programmes, and wield a mighty influence over people. The make-believe world of the haute couture catwalks of Milan, Paris, Tokyo and London are not just places where wild, unaffordable and (in many cases) unwearable fashions are displayed to rich fawning audiences, but they also serve to furnish the mass fashion markets with new ideas.

Money, they say, can buy you a tremendous amount of personal freedom, but it can't buy you happiness, can't buy you love and it certainly can't buy you taste. Who else would fork out over $1,500 for an Issey Miyake inflatable see-through parka or $5,000 for a Zandra Rhodes velvet evening dress complete with punk-style rips, zips and safety pins but people with far more money than discrimination? Including wealthy pop stars such as Madonna, who can afford to

Is it meant to be seductive, or what? Whether experimenting with materials, as in André Courrèges' diseased polyurethane jump suits of 1970 (above), or in shapes, as in Jean-Paul Gaultier's novelty ice-cream cone holders, (opposite), fashion is constantly looking for new ways of turning men off women. Perhaps the whole thing is a joke, but at whose expense - those who pay many thousands of dollars for the originals?

commission Gaultier to design her stage wear, it is estimated that there are now only 3,000 women in the world who can afford the designers' haute couture originals. At prices which start at $3,000 and reach $60,000 for a full-scale evening dress, you don't just have to be obscenely rich to enjoy the top end of fashion but brainless or immoral too. Like a collector of valuable prints or paintings, the highly exclusive, the wearer of limited edition haute couture garments assumes a super-snob status. Too many rich bitches (male and female) hanker after high fashion in the mistaken belief that money and exclusivity are a sign of taste. In many cases they are - bad taste.

But let's be fair, admiration for these purveyors of the unwearable does not stop with the unspeakable. They have large followings, and through the good services of the fashion cognoscenti there is a market eager to see their latest effusions through photographs in newspapers, magazines and on TV. Issey Miyake's 1983 'Bodyworks' exhibition featured huge black silicon models hanging from rafters and draped in paper raincoats, wetsuits and rattan cages. The catalogue showed a photograph of a girl wearing nothing but a shaped plastic breastplate, smoking a cigarette, with the other hand coyly on her crotch. Under it was a quotation from the Master: 'I want to show people how great it is to be free. I want to unwind the threads which bind them.' Kitsch or just killingly funny? Thousands thought neither in Tokyo, Los Angeles, San Francisco and London, where they sat cross-legged on the floor in reverential silence for hours.

Elton John looks like one of the few in the pop world who knows that what they are wearing today will eventually look as ridiculous as what they wore a few years ago.

POP AND FASHION

Contemporary fashion designers can attain pop star status - witness the adulation of an Yves St Laurent or Calvin Klein. However, the relationship between the two businesses is more interesting when going the other way. Because the two worlds are so alike, it is not surprising that we should turn to pop stars for the walking examples of fashion at its most extreme. Enter here a kitsch hero, Elton John.

Where Elton is more interesting than the other fashion leaders of the pop world is his durability. Most stars are linked with the fashions of the brief flickering moment in which they enjoyed their fame. But Elton, always highly noticeably dressed, has managed to keep changing with the times. As he moved from danceable singles to grown-up CDs, his interest with fashion has kept apace.

Very few pop stars have combined their rude taste with a sense of humour in the way that Elton has. He rose to fame in the kitsch hey-day of Glam Rock in the early seventies as a sort of thinking man's

110

Gary Glitter, never taking himself too seriously but always moving ahead of the game. As a younger man, he was an outrageous character, always displaying a well-developed sense of the ridiculous with his attire. As he was a little short-sighted, myopics worldwide immediately identified with him as he boldly went forth in the most outrageous eyewear. His celebrated collection of sunglasses started a fashion for outlandish shades. Elton wore specs with furry frames, ones which spelt out his name in flashing lights, frames that incorporated sea horses, palm trees, bicycle shapes and stars and stripes (his favourite) into the design. The more ridiculous, the better.

A quick glimpse of his stage costumes (many of which he also wore in everyday life) displays his fine sense of vulgarity. You only have to look at his fluorescent balls jumpsuit (made by Bill Whitten in 1973), the imitation mother-of-pearl Statue of Liberty outfit (where he looked exactly like a large kitsch tourist souvenir), or the pink Eiffel Tower boater to appreciate his fine sense of comedy. He celebrated the glitz and pizzazz of glam rock and of Vegas-style showbiz, while gently taking the rise out of it.

These days, rather sadly, Elton seems desperate to prove to the world that he has grown up. In 1988, he got rid of his toys at a huge auction at Sotheby's in London and sold what was probably the most comprehensive collection of kitsch objets d'art. Everything, from cutie-doll radios (complete with see-through negligées) to Andy Warhol and Allen Jones originals went under the hammer.

Like pop hits, today's fashions will inevitably appear to be in very poor taste in just a few years time. We eagerly embrace current fashion styles, but the betting is that one day what you are wearing now will look as ridiculous as cap-sleeve

We all embrace current styles, but the betting is that one day shell suits like this will look as ridiculous as that cap-sleeve T-shirt you're wearing now.

T-shirts and hot pants. Take the current passion for sportswear for example. This has the true kitsch bogus promise in that by donning gear emblazoned with legends such as Reebok, Champion or Russell Athletic, people can identify with those super-fit super-men and women of track and field. But our ordinary physiques or even worse, size 16 sweat shirts and waist 36 sweat pants, just accentuate Michelin-man silhouettes and make athletes of no-one. Watch out weekend shoppers in your shell-suits and air pumps.

COME ON DOWN!

It is sometimes said that in the Western world television is many people's primary experience of the world outside their immediate existence. So with the overwhelming popularity of shows like 'The Black and White Minstrel Show '(above) and 'The Price is Right' (opposite) it is only amazing that cosmic men in white coats have not come to take the planet away.

In 1926 a Scotsman gave the world the first demonstration of a startling invention. His small box with a screen - a 'wireless with pictures' - may have been basic but it was to change everbody's life. Like indoor lavatories, virtually every home now has a television and, in extreme cases, there's a set in every room in the house. If you're frightened about straying too far away from a screen, tiny, hand-held portable televisions are now available so you can enjoy your favourite programmes literally anywhere, including that indoor toilet. In the main living area of most households, this electrical apparatus takes pride of place, furniture is arranged to afford a clear view of the TV and family members will frequently fight over the best seats.

As we have seen throughout this book, the most popular forms of entertainment are the ones most laden with kitsch. Of all these, television is the most avaricious, absorbing other forms of entertainment, and the most shallow, generally offering simply 'light entertainment' (a generic TV term embracing anything that's not factual, seriously dramatic or sports-based). Increasingly, it is nothing more than moving wallpaper.

Broadcasters are motivated by desire for the biggest slice of the audience cake, for the more viewers they can capture, the more they can charge for the advertising space that surrounds and infiltrates the programmes, and thus, the more money they can make. People being what they are, and it being people that watch TV, the product of the struggle between the broadcasting superpowers is not education and edification, but the facile and the tacky - the tickle not the tragic.

As well as consuming other entertainment media, television has spawned a number of genres specifically to fit the restrictive half-hourly basis of its schedules and the desperately meagre audience attention spans. It is these - the game, chat and variety shows, soap operas and situation comedies - that dominate the schedules, and that represent television at its most characteristic. By some quirk of coincidence, they are also the biggest audience pullers.

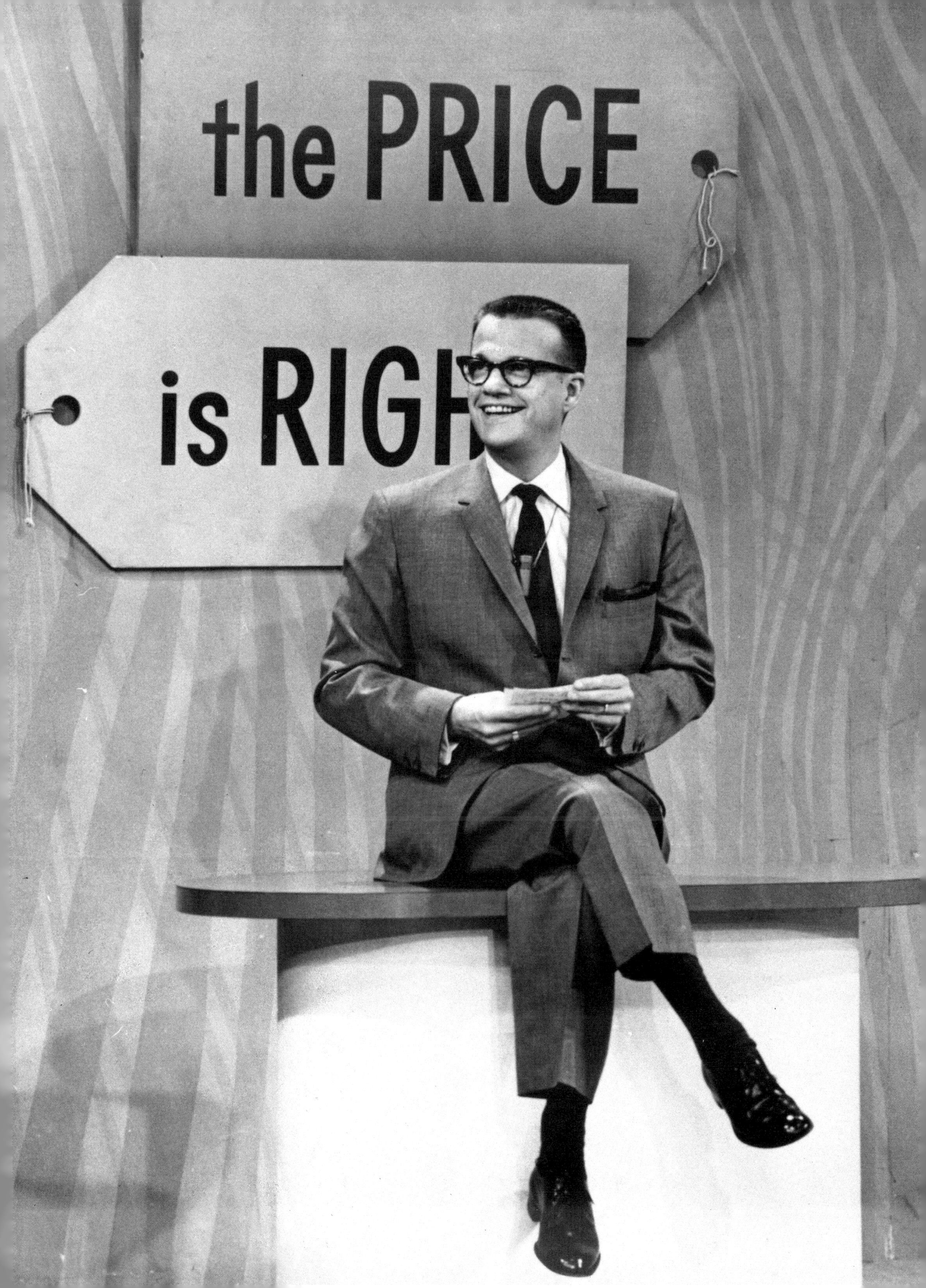
the PRICE
is RIGH

Game shows, soap operas and situation comedies make the three legs of the kitsch tripod that the TV camera most profitably rests upon. Their reward in the after-life is that these are the programmes that most readily find cult audiences when dusted down and rerun in late-night slots. All of them simultaneously exploit and reinforce suburban values; in the case of comedy this is often done by introducing some alien element into a suburban setting, such as in the incongruously hick ways of the Beverly Hillbillies in the hit sixties show of that name.

FOR LOVE AND MONEY

Game-playing has always been hugely popular with TV audiences. In television's infancy in the early fifties, the running was made by shows such as 'Twenty Questions?' and 'What's My Line?', which was estimated to have been watched by up to an incredible 90 per cent of those with television sets. Quiz and panel games were polite, middle-class televisual equivalents of parlour-games like 'Charades'. They were the perfect 'safe' programming in an age that worried about its slip showing.

In the USA, anything suggestive, coarse, or worst of all, vaguely left-wing was censored. Even rock'n'roll was banned from many programmes, and when Elvis finally made it to a grudging 'Ed Sullivan Show' he was only to be shot from the waist up. In the UK the BBC, under the stern supervision of Lord Reith, was considered a strict guardian of morality. Its watchdog, programme chief Cecil

McGivern, issued a memo to producers on 'vulgarity' which warned: 'There is an absolute ban on jokes about lavatories, effeminacy in men, suggestive references to honeymoon couples, chambermaids, fig leaves, ladies' underwear and animal habits (e.g. rabbits).'

Initially American game shows had a nasty populist edge their British counterparts avoided. In 1950 the CBS network launched 'Beat the Clock', in which contestants performed zany stunts against a ticking clock. In the wake of its huge success audiences soon became addicted to game shows that rang, buzzed, gonged, klunked and zonked.

Game shows then became noisier and wilder in a ferociously competitive environment, reaching a consumerist frenzy in 1955 when producer Louis G. Cowan dreamed up a quiz that would showcase 'the common man with uncommon knowledge'. This was an adaptation in an appropriately inflated five figures of a radio success ('The $64 Question') - 'The $64,000 Question'. Not only did this programme donate a new cliché to the English language, but it became a national sensation. It was claimed that while the show was on, America's crime rate dropped, as did movie, baseball and bingo attendances. The programme's trademarks were isolation booths, tension music and plateaux which allowed the contestants a week to consider whether they would risk all for the next question.

Naturally, this success spawned dozens of imitations. To ward off the competition, the show's producers began giving money away to

Although decried as bad taste at the time, the early game shows such as 'What's My Line' seem like polite parlour games set next to the noisy, brash and banal consumerism of what was to come later.

contestants by the truckload. One contestant walked off with the highest amount ever won on a quiz show, a staggering $264,000!!!

Somewhat inevitably, this uncontrolled extravagance was to lead eventually down kitsch's familiar kitsch path of corruption and outrage, and 'The $64,000 Question' was pulled from the schedules in 1958 in a series of scandals surrounding several rival quiz shows. It was not, however, this programme but NBC's 'Twenty-One' that knocked down the whole house of cards, when it was revealed that a young contestant, Charles Van Doren, had cheated. The show's producers had provided him with answers and ad-libs and coached him to hesitate, stammer and pat his brow to build suspense. The networks, of course, declared their ignorance of all such goings on but cancelled all remaining big money quizzes and refused to hire anybody connected with them, including NBC's new anchor man... Charles Van Doren.

Meanwhile, on the other side of the Atlantic, the game show monster was only in its infancy. When ITV (dismissed by Winston Churchill as a 'tuppenny Punch and Judy Show' even before it started) began transmitting in 1955, previously polite pieces of electrical apparatus burst forth with boisterous quizzes modelled on American originals. 'Double Your Money', 'Take Your Pick' and 'Criss-Cross Quiz' were the first British game shows to give cash prizes. They were also the forefathers that begat the brash and rude game shows that proliferate today.

Game shows fill the airwaves because they are cheap to produce - and it shows - even if the prizes are quite lavish. The only 'professional' needed is some vacuous ex-holiday camp entertainer or fading comedian to act as a presenter, and the only talent they need is to be able to turn on a cheesy smile and slap people on the back without leaving too visible a damp patch. The rest of the cast is made up of willing members of the public with skin as thick as a rhinoceros' and an IQ somewhat lower. Many of the prizes are often comically inappropriate, with tower-block dwellers winning sets of garden furniture which, however you look at them, won't squeeze into window boxes, or little old ladies struggling to take home windsurfers. Kitsch fans love the shows - the brasher the better.

The very best of trash game shows are the classics from the past, as somehow their idiocies seem merely naivety, like all the indiscretions of our youth. Those with the most convoluted rules and the most unpleasant hosts prove the most enduring: 'Queen for a Day' was widely criticised as a vulgar exploitation of human misery in an orgy of commercial plugs. Nevertheless, it was a number one daytime

heesey, insincere smiles and a smarmy patronising of guests and the viewing audiences are trademarks of the game show host the world over. Bob Monkhouse has been honing his skills on British audiences since the genre first spread (on shipborne rats?) across the Atlantic in the fifties.

show first on American radio, then on TV, running for nearly 20 years between 1945 and 1964. Five contestants were plucked from the audience each day to compete for the title of 'Queen' and the accompanying raft of prizes by telling, usually through tears, why they wanted a particular item. Always behind the need was a personal story of some pathos, but some of the wishes were tragic - one contestant wanted an urn to bury her mother, another a new artificial eye for her husband as his last one had frozen and cracked!

The game show with the highest decibel count and the most materialistic goals was 'The Price is Right' - popular on US TV in the late fifties and revived in 1972 with Bill Cullen as the original MC. In this show the required skill was knowing the price of household goods. A British version was launched in 1984 with presenter Leslie Crowther calling 'Come on down!' over blaring music to people picked from hysterical hooligan audiences tantalised by the sight of 'the lovely Carole' draped across a lawnmower or a cocktail cabinet. Only one contestant refused to come on down - on the very first show.

Game shows are noisy, vulgar and filled with bad taste and this is why they are so successful - it is what the general public wants. And they're not all about money; in the sixties 'love' had become so popular that it began to rival cash and consumer goods in pulling in the audiences. In 1966 ABC ran 'The Dating Game' in which the prizes were not wheelbarrows full of greenbacks or cuddly toys but partners!

The Price is Right plumbed depths previous shows had not even sailed over. Originally hosted on US television in the fifties by Bill Cullen (see p.113), it featured an hysterical audience competing ferociously in a frenzy of consumerism, and the only skill it required was knowing the price of household goods. Leslie Crowther did the honours when British TV knew it could resist it no longer.

This spawned a sibling in 'The Newlyweds Game' in which freshly married couples were quizzed as to how well they had gotten to know their partners in the short space of their courtship. This in turn inspired a geriatric version in Britain - 'Mr and Mrs', a torpid game show for wrinklies, which had the insipid Derek Batey as host. This particular game show sub-genre is enormously popular again today. From the mid-eighties kitsch fans in Britain have been able to sate themselves with the UK's own version of 'The Dating Game' - Cilla Black's blatantly staged 'Blind Date'. Week in, week out, the public is riveted to its sofa seats by the the squirm value of contestants providing lewd answers to risque questions from unseen partners-to-be, and candidly passing judgement on their blind dates.

DESPERATELY SEEKING TALENT

The public has a great desire to appear on television. They can do this by being quickly glimpsed as part of a studio audience, a contestant in one of the afore-mentioned game shows or they may try (God forbid!) to gain their 15 minutes of fame on one of the many TV talent shows that have appeared, disappeared and re-appeared on our screens over the years.

The US networks ran several barmy contests in the fifties for such talents as 'Newsboy of the Year', and 'Amateur Hours' have been popular on the smaller cable networks. But, taking its inspiration from these shows, the one that put more mediocrity on TV than any other over the years was the BBC's 'Opportunity Knocks'. Between 1956 and 1977 it produced acts of the calibre of Bobby Crush, Bonnie Langford, Peters and Lee, the singing miners Millican and Nesbitt, Neil Reid and Lena Zavaroni.

Out of the thousands of acts auditioned, only a handful have proved bearable - like Les Dawson and Mary Hopkin. A small point of interest here is that kitsch curiosity, singer Englebert Humperdinck (then known as plain old Gerry Dorsey) failed the auditions (maybe they had some judgement, after all)! In the early seventies (this was a classic period for kitsch, remember?) the public couldn't get enough of these dreadful shows. 'New Faces', ITV's equivalent, differed only in that it had the added spice of a panel of showbiz 'experts'. The panel would make (often brutal) comments about the acts and award scores for such attributes as 'Presentation', 'Content' and last, and in most cases sadly lacking, 'Star Quality'.

At about the same time as 'New Faces' appeared on UK screens a more brutal public exercise of judgement on raw and untried talent TV began on American TV, Chuck Barriss's 'The Gong Show'. Originally a daytime cheapie, it graduated onto the prime-time schedules in 1976 on NBC. Oddball and freak acts were invited to perform before a celebrity panel that dismissed those that failed to please it in mid-performance by striking a gong.

Not only supremely banal but also positively tacky is the 'Miss World' contest. This supposed beauty contest is certainly up-market from the tacky 'Mother and Daughter Beauty Contests' that were popular on US TV in the fifties, but 'Miss World' is now considered by TV bosses as too sexist for British screens (although it is still shown throughout the rest of the world). The competition was the brainchild of a legendarily arrogant impresario, Eric Morley (a dab hand at tacky TV, being the man behind the comically antiquated ballroom dancing contests, 'Come Dancing'). 'Miss World' appeals to the mentality of the male bigot, whose ideal is a firm, young female, a mindless bimbo with an hourglass figure who won't talk back.

DRAMA BY THE BATHTUB

Soap operas invariably top the TV ratings charts. Absolutely massive audiences tune in each week and events such as weddings, deaths and scandals can set entire nations talking.

Like the game show, the soap opera is another American

Meat-market beauty contests such as 'Miss World' prove the oft-mooted adage that the only people more stupid than those who watch such programmes are those who appear on them.

invention, a form of entertainment tailored to the audience's short attention span and craving for excitement. TV soaps are a follow-on from the long-running US radio serials of the thirties such as 'Pepper Young's Family' and 'When a Girl Marries', which commanded huge followings before the days of the universal cathode ray tube.

These serialised stories are followed eagerly by dedicated viewers on either a weekly, alternate daily or even daily basis. Although some soaps do valiantly attempt to reflect life and deal with topical social problems, the majority are little more than comic-strip stories with characters that the audience love to identify with, or love to hate. Like game shows, soaps are good news for the TV companies because they are cheap to produce, and they deliver audiences.

It didn't take long for the public to develop a soapy addiction. Prime-time soaps such as 'Peyton Place' in America and 'Coronation Street' in Britain began transmission in the early sixties and created a gold rush like the one 10 years earlier for game shows. Rival networks, never ones to miss out on a really bad idea, created all sorts of trash in their hustle and bustle for a piece of the action. The very worst of soaps make the best viewing today. These are the ones which not only suffer from having too little budget and insufficient time spent on them, but are made by a cast and crew who appear never to have passed their TV production proficiency tests. The truth is that the programme makers know full well that once they've got an audience hooked, they'll never notice the shortcomings.

The most loved and best-remembered ropey soap on British TV

Pop and TV have always needed each other. Agnetha, Bjorn, Benny and Annafried – better known as Swedish seventies megastars ABBA – were propelled to international stardom on the 'Eurovision Song Contest' in 1974. This annual parade of the lowest common denominators in musical invention claims a Europe-wide audience of hundreds of millions. Since its institution in 1956 it has given the Continent a new Euro-language, best illustrated by such song titles as 'La, La, La, Ding Ding a Dong', 'Boom Bang-a-Bang' and 'A-Ba-Ni-Bi'.

was 'Crossroads', which until it was killed off after 24 years in 1988 was one of the country's favourite jokes. This programme centred on a widow Meg Richardson and her two children who turned the family home into a motel. Originally scheduled to run for only six weeks, 'Crossroads' became as much a part of British life as waiting to be served at Woolworth's. Radio Rentals brought out an advertisement for a video recorder which promised: 'It can take 16 episodes of "Crossroads" (if you can!)'. Comedians cracked jokes about 'Crossroads' actors being sacked for remembering their lines. The quality of the acting did improve with time but the plots didn't.

To its credit, 'Crossroads' did try to deal with controversial issues such as Down's Syndrome, abortion, rape, racism and test-tube pregnancy, but like any soap, due to the pressures of having to come up with enough stories to keep the audienced addicted, any major character has to go through in a matter of years what the rest of us would be hard crammed to push into 20 lifetimes! Meg Richardson's daughter, Jill, the only surviving cast member from the first episode to the last, was married three times (once bigamously), had a child by her step-brother, became a drug addict, an alcoholic and, for good measure had a couple of nervous breakdowns. Not that Meg fared much better. Her first husband tried to poison her, she was jailed for dangerous driving, suffered amnesia, and when she thought she'd found true happiness by marrying a successful businessman, he was promptly kidnapped by a gang of international terrorists, and died of a heart-attack. Meg decided that the best thing to do was to sail off on the QE2!

Viewers become hooked to all kinds of utter drivel, and very lovely rubbish some of it is too. The laughably poor standards of 'Crossroads' have largely gone from British and American soaps - most of which now have achieved production values more akin to TV drama. But there are crude equivalents to be found in the proliferating Australian soap opera imports such as 'Neighbours', 'Young Doctors', 'Home and Away' and, best of all, 'Prisoner Cell Block H' - which is a kitsch cult hit in many countries. Set in a women's prison, it has a largely diesel-dyke cast and deals in a brutally unsympathetic light with the sort of issues that you'd expect to get in a women's prison - lesbianism, theft and insecurity. It is all acted and produced with a wonderful first-year film school crudity.

At the opposite end of the soap spectrum lies the ostentatious kitsch of the Ritch-Bitch variety. Had Shakespeare been alive in 1978, he'd have loved J.R. Ewing, the Iago of Dallas, hero of a soap opera

Like the game show, the soap opera has been designed for the shallow attention span of the TV audience. It is those that look as if they were made without the benefit of money by a production crew that flunked film school that are most appreciated by aficionados. The best-loved British ropey soap is 'Crossroads': (right) Meg Richardson (Noële Gordon), Jill Richardson (Jane Rossiter) and Sandy Richardson (Roger Tonge).

121

that was to dominate the soap scene for more than a decade and to prove conclusively that Americans are superior - they wear stetson hats without embarrassment, for example. 'Dallas' was the antithesis of 'Crossroads'. Made on 35mm film like a Hollywood movie, it was the glossiest, most luxurious soap ever seen. The saga of the oil-rich Ewing family was big and brash, just like Texas itself.

The characters were all obscenely wealthy, and the lavish dream-world they inhabited proved irresistible to audiences eager to escape from the drab mundanity of everyday life. The women, with their perfect make-up day and night, made other television heroines look drab, and the continuing crimes of J.R. made other villains look cissies. 'Dallas' proved such a world-wide money-spinner that an inevitable crop of inferior copies and spin-offs sprang up, such as 'Dynasty' (full of rapidly-ageing British screen queens such as Joan Collins, Stephanie Beecham and Kate O'Mara), 'Falcon Crest' (a wine-growing saga made by the 'Dallas' producers, starring Ronald Reagan's ex-wife Jane Wyman as an all-conquering boss) and 'The Colbys'. At least these had a glossy slickness, but the hammy 'Santa Barbara' returned us to the amateurish standards of the Eisenhower years.

But even an all-star cast and top production values couldn't disguise the fact at the end of the day 'Dallas' and co. were just very well-dressed dross, with plots as dire as the amateur dramatics of their predecessors. For example, in 'Dallas' in 1985 Patrick Duffy, the actor who played J.R.'s brother, Bobby, decided not to renew his contract. The writers had him killed off. Ratings fell dramatically and simultaneously, Duffy decided that there was no life after soap. However, in soap there can be life after death as the 'Dallas' producers proved. The actor received a pay rise, Bobby came back from the dead by materialising in his wife's shower and his disappearance was written off as her dream! Surely viewers would not stand for such cynical manipulation. They could, and they did, and although 'Dallas' never made the world giddy again it still bubbled on for a few more years.

THAT RICH, INEXHAUSTIBLE COMEDY
OF SUBURBAN LIFE

Like the soap opera, the situation comedy is a direct descendant of a radio show formula. The first TV sitcom dates back to 1951 with Lucille Ball's 'I Love Lucy'. This was one of the first comedy shows to be recorded with three cameras simultaneously in front of a live audience. What the audience was privileged to spy on was a slapstick comedy in which Lucy and her hubbie (played by real-life husband

Desi Arnez) are a couple whose life was full of madcap shenanigans such as Lucy filling their apartment full of soap-suds. This show proved to be the most enormous success, topping the CBS ratings for many years. It set the tone for most sit-coms for the years to come as a televisual version of the theatrical farce.

This has been a staple form of TV comedy ever since, but today it is a very tired-looking format. TV schedules are littered with hundreds of such shows but, unfortunately, bad situation comedy does not have the same appeal to the kitsch fan that crass soap operas, game shows or talent competitions do. With their lame humour and unimaginative settings, they are mostly merely unwatchable. Bad comedy just fails to amuse.

The Hollywood-style big budget production values of the glossy soaps of the eighties like 'Dallas' and 'Dynasty' don't disguise the fact that they are just well-dressed dross, with plots and situations no better than the amateur dramatics of their cheapo sisters. The truth can now be told: 'Dynasty' (left) was, in fact, planned entirely as a huge charitable project to resuscitate the careers of ageing semi-stars Joan Collins, Stephanie Beecham and Kate O'Mara.

However, in contrast to drab and grey unfunny modern sitcoms, there are stacks of bizarre and imaginative shows from the fifties and sixties which are just packed with funny ideas. They now enjoy a huge popularity with TV trash-loving folk.

'The Addams Family' and 'The Munsters' were about two families of suburban ghouls whose members had more than passing resemblances to horror characters such as Frankenstein and Dracula. 'Bewitched' was about a mother and daughter who are both witches. The daughter is married to an advertising man who is forever trying to get her to give up witchcraft for him but her mother keeps pulling her back. 'I Dream of Jeannie' featured 'Dallas' star-to-be Larry Hagman playing a shipwrecked astronaut who pulled out a cork from a bottle one day and out popped a female genie, called Jeannie, ready to do her master's bidding. The trouble is she misunderstands just about everything he orders and her presence is incredibly difficult to explain to people. The odd mixture of suburbia and the supernatural give these typical views of suburban life a compelling quality.

There are a lot of old TV comedy programmes that are enjoyed by people in the same way that old kitsch pop is appreciated - the passing of time has had a distancing effect so that TV once dismissed as the trash of your childhood or youth can now be celebrated as kitsch. These shows that were once tea-time favourites for kiddies are now re-run on the late-night TV shows for those same now-grown-up kids. Some big faves are 'The Partridge Family' - an often yukkily sentimental show about a family (with movie actress Shirley Jones as mom and teeny-idol David Cassidy as big brother) who were shouldering the burden of rough times as a touring pop group - 'Thunderbirds' - a sort of James Bond spoof with strings - and 'Pinky and Perky' - two squeaky, singing piglet puppets who cavorted around singing, or rather squealing, the hits of the day. They were the sort of characters who made you think that the Big Bad Wolf wasn't such a bad guy after all.

The cuddly and soggy amiability of 'I Love Lucy' (above) set the tone for a slew of sitcoms that followed through the fifties and sixties. Repeats of Lucy's well-intentioned bumbling still bring the warm sensation that there is nothing done in the world so bad that a shrug of the shoulders will not forgive it.

THE WACKY AND WEIRD

Scores of science fiction series have been produced in TV's 30-odd-year history. Some were intelligent, some had incredible special effects and some were haunting or funny. The earliest appear naive, even bumbling by today's standards, guaranteeing large audiences for re-runs of series such as 'Get Smart!', 'The Invisible Man', and 'Dr Who'.

These shows were mostly concerned with things 'not-of-this-earth', space travel and seeing into the future (like themes evident within the designs of many household furnishings of the time) and now seem even less-of-this-earth than ever before. Of these shows, 'My Favourite Martian' has one of the most absurd settings. A Martian anthropologist with a vast array of powers is stranded on earth - in Las Vegas, no less, where a newspaperman takes him under his wing and passes him off as his uncle, keeping his Martian identity secret and his antennae under his hat! Or perhaps it's not so absurd; is Vegas on the same planet as the rest of us?

The shows that keep cropping up time and time again the world over are mainly the brainchildren of one Rod Serling, a favourite figure for enthusiasts of this small-screen genre. He was the creator, principal writer and co-producer of 'The Twilight Zone', a fantasy-anthology series which debuted in 1959. He also appeared to introduce the story each week, when his eerie on-screen presence gave an air of semi-solid reality to the bizarre stories which followed. These reliably wacky science fiction half-hour yarns transported loyal fans to the sixth dimension each week for five years and Serling became American television's most celebrated writer. He was also responsible for another weirdo TV series, 'Night Gallery', which began in 1970 and was

Dick Yorke and Elizabeth Montgomery with the baby Tabatha in 'Bewitched' (above) and (left) the cast of 'The Munsters'. Depicting in their different ways what happens when the supernatural encounters suburbia, both programmes show suburban values winning on a knock-out every time.

Serling's venture into the occult. This time, each show opened with him in an art gallery after closing time. He would begin his narration by strolling past the pictures, then pause at one which represented the evening's story such as a terrifying portrait of a creature prowling around a cemetery. The frame would then dissolve into action...

TRASH BY DESIGN

Like pop music, in order constantly to come up with new ideas, the television business feeds on itself. 'Monty Python' began sending up the conventions in a surrealistic manner back in the late sixties. Today, trashy television has proved so popular that many programme-makers think that the answer is to create trash deliberately, but it requires genius intentionally to make the unfunny funny, and the programmes usually flop. What the producers fail to understand is that a fundamental part of the appeal of kitsch is that it is produced in the first place for a public that actually quite likes it at face value. Other people's bad taste, remember?

Another tack has been to celebrate crass and embarrassing moments on TV. Shows like 'Bloopers' in the USA, and 'Clive James on Television' and 'It'll be All Right on the Night' in the UK, are largely made up of out-takes, mistakes and fluffed lines, but they also include a smattering of bizarre examples of what people in other countries consider entertainment, but which to the show's hosts seem unimitigatingly awful. A favourite target is Japanese TV game shows such as the now-legendary 'Endurance'. This piece of family viewing tests which contestants can endure the most vile tortures longest, such as having to hold their heads underwater in a rockpool of carniverous fish. Creating entertainment by laughing at foreigners and their misplaced ideas of fun can be OK, but at the same time there is something irritatingly smug about these shows too.

It may not be possible to re-create kitsch TV but it has been skillfully satirised on many occasions. In 1978, the American writer-producer Susan Harris created 'Soap', a wonderfully funny send up of daytime American soap operas. Featuring life with the Campbell family, it incorporated homosexuality, religion, sex, aliens and senility - often in the same episode. Character-comedian Barry Humphries has developed his alter ego Dame Edna Everage into a figure who is far better known now than he is under his own name. Intended as an affront to polite British taste, his brash and bawdy oversized Australian

Dame Edna Everage – once a shaft aimed at public expectations of the stars and the mass values that underlie them, now she is in danger of becoming the kitsch that starts off by sending itself up only to end up by becoming a yet more baroque form of kitsch. Kitsch is very difficult to satirise, as many ponderous and unfunny attempts have proved. One of the most successful attempts was the long-running TV soap, 'Soap'(Left).

bears testimony to the trend to institutionalise kitsch. She has become a huge celebrity in her own right by flaunting the very characteristics that are supposed to make us squirm, and the famous of stage, screen and politics have voluntarily lined up to be humiliated on her own versions of chat programmes and variety shows.

WHITHER NOW?

TV's powerful grip on us now seems no less tight. The average American or Brit spends well over 20 hours a week watching the mesmeric little screen. And with some quaint die-hards spending their leisure hours following alternative pursuits like reading books, playing football or building model aeroplanes, that average means that much of the population is spending nearly as much time with the TV set as they do at work.

Kitsch lovers like TV for having seen through it. When the Bay City Rollers record has finished at that dinner party, they put on a videotape of 'Captain Scarlet'. Whether the rest of the population will follow remains to be seen, but perhaps the passion for showing old programmes will merge with the fashion for showing old videos, and the TV executives will realise that only news and sport will ever offer anything new. We can then all settle down to a celebration of TV's tinselly past. But whatever happens, this ultimately populist medium will continue to behave in a way which would have the seventeenth-century formulaters of 'good taste' reaching for their zap buttons. Get into sync with kitsch, for you can't escape!

What better way to wrap up a kitsch dinner party than to settle down to a session of underwater entertainment from that aquatic superhero marionette, Troy Tempest and the mute beauty Marina, in Gerry Anderson's classic puppet TV series 'Stingray'?